Raymond Williams was born in 1921 at the
Welsh border village of Pandy. Educated at
Abergavenny Grammar School and at Trinity
College, Cambridge, he saw war service as an
anti-tank captain in the Guards Armoured
Division. After the war he was appointed an
adult education tutor in the Oxford University
Delegacy for Extra-Mutal studies. In 1961 he
was elected Fellow of Jesus College, Cambridge,
and he is now university Reader in Drama.
In 1973 he was Professor of Political Science
in Stanford University, California. His published
books include *Drama in Performance, Culture
and Society 1780-1950, The Long Revolution,
Communications, Modern Tragedy, Border Country,
Second Generation, The English Novel from Dickens
to Lawrence, Keywords* and *The Country and
the City*. He is also the author of *Orwell* in
Fontana's *Modern Masters* series, and the general
editor of the Fontana *Communications* series.

D0619107

TECHNOSPHERE

Technosphere is a series that presents individual studies of particular sciences and technologies in terms of their human repercussions. The series will include original analyses of a wide variety of subjects with the emphasis in each case on the present state of the science or technology in question, its social significance, and the future direction of its probable and necessary development.

The series editor is Jonathan Benthall, author of *Science and Technology in Art Today* and *The Body Electric: Patterns of Western Industrial Culture*, editor of *Ecology: the Shaping Enquiry* and *The Limits of Human Nature*, and co-editor of *The Body as a Medium of Expression*. Formerly lecture programme organizer at the Institute of Contemporary Arts, he is now Director of the Royal Anthropological Institute.

Also published
Alternative Technology and the Politics of Technical Change, *David Dickson*
The Medicine You Take, *D. R. Laurence and J. W. Black*

Television

Technology and Cultural Form

RAYMOND WILLIAMS

FONTANA/COLLINS

First published in Fontana 1974
Second Impression April 1974
Third Impression August 1978
Fourth Impression August 1979
Copyright © Raymond Williams 1974

Made and printed in Great Britain by
William Collins Sons & Co Ltd, Glasgow

Contents

Foreword

This book is an attempt to explore and describe some of the relationships between television as a technology and television as a cultural form. In the contemporary debate about the general relations between technology, social institutions and culture, television is obviously an outstanding case. Indeed its present importance, as an element in each of these areas, and as a point of interaction between them, is in effect unparalleled.

I have been meaning to attempt this inquiry since I wrote *The Long Revolution* and *Communications*, which were more closely concerned with the cultural institutions of print. As in those earlier studies, the social history and the social analysis needed to be directly related to critical and analytical examination of the materials and processes of the specific communication. Over four years, from 1968 to 1972, I wrote a monthly review of television for the BBC weekly journal *The Listener*. I was able to choose my own subjects and on several occasions tried to sum up my impressions of a particular television use or form – sport, travel, police serials, commercials, political reporting, discussions. These articles are a necessary background for the present inquiry, and I have drawn on some of their experience for this book, which was, however, mainly written in California, in a very different television situation. I have taken the opportunity to make some comparisons between British and American practice. I also took the opportunity of discussion with colleagues in the Department of Communications at Stanford University and was especially helped by some of their work on new and emerging television technologies. I am

Television

especially grateful to Edwin B. Parker, and for discussions elsewhere to Mr Rice of KQED San Francisco, to Dr John Fekete,
to Mr Nicholas Garnham and to my son Dr Ederyn Williams.
My wife's work on the material for Chapters Three, Four and
Six was at once primary and indispensable. I am also grateful
to Mr Jonathan Benthall for his help throughout the inquiry.

Stanford, California,
and Cambridge, England.
January–June, 1973.

8

1. The technology and the society

It is often said that television has altered our world. In the same way, people often speak of a new world, a new society, a new phase of history, being created – 'brought about' – by this or that new technology: the steam-engine, the automobile, the atomic bomb. Most of us know what is generally implied when such things are said. But this may be the central difficulty: that we have got so used to statements of this general kind, in our most ordinary discussions, that we can fail to realise their specific meanings.

For behind all such statements lie some of the most difficult and most unresolved historical and philosophical questions. Yet the questions are not posed by the statements; indeed they are ordinarily masked by them. Thus we often discuss, with animation, this or that 'effect' of television, or the kinds of social behaviour, the cultural and psychological conditions, which television has 'led to', without feeling ourselves obliged to ask whether it is reasonable to describe any technology as a cause, or, if we think of it as a cause, as what kind of cause, and in what relations with other kinds of causes. The most precise and discriminating local study of 'effects' can remain superficial if we have not looked into the notions of cause and effect, as between a technology and a society, a technology and a culture, a technology and a psychology, which underlie our questions and may often determine our answers.

It can of course be said that these fundamental questions are very much too difficult; and that they are indeed difficult is very soon obvious to anyone who tries to follow them through. We could spend our lives trying to answer them, whereas here and now, in a society in which television is important, there is immediate and practical work to be done: surveys to be made, research undertaken; surveys and research, moreover, which we know how to do. It is an appealing position, and it has the advantage, in our kind of society, that it is understood as practical, so that it can then be supported and funded. By contrast, other kinds of question seem merely theoretical and abstract.

Yet all questions about cause and effect, as between a technology and a society, are intensely practical. Until we have begun to answer them, we really do not know, in any particular case, whether, for example, we are talking about a technology or about the uses of a technology; about necessary institutions or particular and changeable institutions; about a content or about a form. And this is not only a matter of intellectual uncertainty; it is a matter of social practice. If the technology is a cause, we can at best modify or seek to control its effects. Or if the technology, as used, is an effect, to what other kinds of cause, and other kinds of action, should we refer and relate our experience of its uses? These are not abstract questions. They form an increasingly important part of our social and cultural arguments, and they are being decided all the time in real practice, by real and effective decisions.

It is with these problems in mind that I want to try to analyse television as a particular cultural technology, and to look at its development, its institutions, its forms and its effects, in this critical dimension. In the present chapter, I shall begin the analysis under three headings: (a) versions of cause and effect in technology and society; (b) the social history of television as a technology; (c) the social history of the uses of television technology.

A. VERSIONS OF CAUSE AND EFFECT IN TECHNOLOGY AND SOCIETY

We can begin by looking again at the general statement that

television has altered our world. It is worth setting down some of the different things this kind of statement has been taken to mean. For example:

(i) Television was invented as a result of scientific and technical research. Its power as a medium of news and entertainment was then so great that it altered all preceding media of news and entertainment.

(ii) Television was invented as a result of scientific and technical research. Its power as a medium of social communication was then so great that it altered many of our institutions and forms of social relationships.

(iii) Television was invented as a result of scientific and technical research. Its inherent properties as an electronic medium altered our basic perceptions of reality, and thence our relations with each other and with the world.

(iv) Television was invented as a result of scientific and technical research. As a powerful medium of communication and entertainment it took its place with other factors – such as greatly increased physical mobility, itself the result of other newly invented technologies – in altering the scale and form of our societies.

(v) Television was invented as a result of scientific and technical research, and developed as a medium of entertainment and news. It then had unforeseen consequences, not only on other entertainment and news media, which it reduced in viability and importance, but on some of the central processes of family, cultural and social life.

(vi) Television, discovered as a possibility by scientific and technical research, was selected for investment and development to meet the needs of a new kind of society, especially in the provision of centralised entertainment and in the centralised formation of opinions and styles of behaviour.

(vii) Television, discovered as a possibility by scientific and technical research, was selected for investment and promotion as a new and profitable phase of a domestic consumer economy; it is then one of the characteristic 'machines for the home'.

(viii) Television became available as a result of scientific and technical research, and in its character and uses exploited and emphasised elements of a passivity, a cultural and psychological inadequacy, which had always been latent in people, but which television now organised and came to represent.

(ix) Television became available as a result of scientific and technical research, and in its character and uses both served and exploited the needs of a new kind of large-scale and complex but atomised society.

These are only some of the possible glosses on the ordinary bald statement that television has altered our world. Many people hold mixed versions of what are really alternative opinions, and in some cases there is some inevitable overlapping. But we can distinguish between two broad classes of opinion.

In the first – (i) to (v) – the technology is in effect accidental. Beyond the strictly internal development of the technology there is no reason why any particular invention should have come about. Similarly it then has consequences which are also in the true sense accidental, since they follow directly from the technology itself. If television had not been invented, this argument would run, certain definite social and cultural events would not have occurred.

In the second – (vi) to (ix) – television is again, in effect, a technological accident, but its significance lies in its uses, which are held to be symptomatic of some order of society or some qualities of human nature which are otherwise determined. If television had not been invented, this argument runs, we would still be manipulated or mindlessly entertained, but in some other way and perhaps less powerfully.

For all the variations of local interpretation and emphasis, these two classes of opinion underlie the overwhelming majority of both professional and amateur views of the effects of television. What they have in common is the fundamental form of the statement: 'television has altered our world'.

It is then necessary to make a further theoretical distinction. The first class of opinion, described above, is that usually known, at least to its opponents, as *technological determinism*. It is an immensely powerful and now largely orthodox view of the nature of social change. New technologies are discovered, by an essentially internal process of research and development, which then sets the conditions for social change and progress. Progress, in particular, is the history of these inventions, which 'created the modern world'. The effects of the technologies, whether direct or indirect, foreseen or unforeseen, are as it were the rest of history. The steam engine, the automobile, television, the atomic bomb, have *made* modern man and the modern condition.

The second class of opinion appears less determinist. Television, like any other technology, becomes available as an element or a medium in a process of change that is in any case occurring or about to occur. By contrast with pure technological determinism, this view emphasises other causal factors in social change. It then considers particular technologies, or a complex of technologies, as *symptoms* of change of some other kind. Any particular technology is then as it were a by-product of a social process that is otherwise determined. It only acquires effective status when it is used for purposes which are already contained in this known social process.

The debate between these two general positions occupies the greater part of our thinking about technology and society. It is a real debate, and each side makes important points. But it is in the end sterile, because each position, though in different ways, has abstracted technology from society. In *technological determinism*, research and development have been assumed as self-generating. The new technologies are invented as it were in an independent sphere, and then create new societies or new human conditions. The view of *symptomatic technology*, similarly, assumes that research and development are self-generating, but in a more marginal way. What is discovered in the margin is then taken up and used.

Each view can then be seen to depend on the isolation of technology. It is either a self-acting force which creates new ways of life, or it is a self-acting force which provides materials for new ways of life. These positions are so deeply established, in modern social thought, that it is very difficult to think beyond them. Most histories of technology, like most histories of scientific discovery, are written from their assumptions. An appeal to 'the facts', against this or that interpretation, is made very difficult simply because the histories are usually written, consciously or unconsciously, to illustrate the assumptions. This is either explicit, with the consequential interpretation attached, or more often implicit, in that the history of technology or of scientific development is offered as a history on its own. This can be seen as a device of specialisation or of emphasis, but it then necessarily implies merely internal intentions and criteria.

To change these emphases would require prolonged and co-operative intellectual effort. But in the particular case of television it may be possible to outline a different kind of interpretation, which would allow us to see not only its history but also its uses in a more radical way. Such an interpretation would differ from technological determinism in that it would restore *intention* to the process of research and development. The technology would be seen, that is to say, as being looked for and developed with certain purposes and practices already in mind. At the same time the interpretation would differ from symptomatic technology in that these purposes and practices would be seen as *direct*: as known social needs, purposes and practices to which the technology is not marginal but central.

B. THE SOCIAL HISTORY OF TELEVISION AS A TECHNOLOGY

The invention of television was no single event or series of events. It depended on a complex of inventions and developments in electricity, telegraphy, photography and motion pictures, and radio. It can be said to have separated out as a specific technological objective in the period 1875–1890, and then, after a lag, to have developed as a specific technological enterprise from 1920 through to the first public television systems of the 1930s. Yet in each of these stages it depended for parts of its realisation on inventions made with other ends primarily in view.

Until the early nineteenth century, investigations of electricity, which had long been known as a phenomenon, were primarily philosophical: investigations of a puzzling natural effect. The technology associated with these investigations was mainly directed towards isolation and concentration of the effect, for its clearer study. Towards the end of the eighteenth century there began to be applications, characteristically in relation to other known natural effects (lightning conductors). But there is then a key transitional period in a cluster of inventions between 1800 and 1831, ranging from Volta's battery to Faraday's demonstration of electro-magnetic induction, leading quickly to the production of generators. This can be properly traced as a scientific history, but it is significant that the key period of advance coincides with an important stage of the development of industrial production. The advantages of electric power were closely related to new industrial needs: for mobility and transfer in the location of power sources, and for flexible and rapid controllable conversion. The steam engine had been well suited to textiles, and its industries had been based on local siting. A more extensive development, both physically and in the complexity of multiple-part processes, such as engineering, could be attempted with other power sources but could only be fully realised with electricity. There was a very complex interaction between new needs and new inventions, at the level of primary production, of new applied industries (plating) and of new social needs which were themselves related to industrial development (city and house lighting). From 1830 to large-scale generation in the 1880s there was this continuing complex of need and invention and application.

In telegraphy the development was simpler. The transmission

of messages by beacons and similar primary devices had been long established. In the development of navigation and naval warfare the flag-system had been standardised in the course of the sixteenth and seventeenth centuries. During the Napoleonic wars there was a marked development of land telegraphy, by semaphore stations, and some of this survived into peacetime. Electrical telegraphy had been suggested as a technical system as early as 1753, and was actually demonstrated in several places in the early nineteenth century. An English inventor in 1816 was told that the Admiralty was not interested. It is interesting that it was the development of the railways, themselves a response to the development of an industrial system and the related growth of cities, which clarified the need for improved telegraphy. A complex of technical possibilities was brought to a working system from 1837 onwards. The development of international trade and transport brought rapid extensions of the system, including the transatlantic cable in the 1850s and the 1860s. A general system of electric telegraphy had been established by the 1870s, and in the same decade the telephone system began to be developed, in this case as a new and intended invention.

In photography, the idea of light-writing had been suggested by (among others) Wedgwood and Davy in 1802, and the *camera obscura* had already been developed. It was not the projection but the fixing of images which at first awaited technical solution, and from 1816 (Niepce) and through to 1839 (Daguerre) this was worked on, together with the improvement of camera devices. Professional and then amateur photography spread rapidly, and reproduction and then transmission, in the developing newspaper press, were achieved. By the 1880s the idea of a 'photographed reality' – still more for record than for observation – was familiar.

The idea of moving pictures had been similarly developing. The magic lantern (slide projection) had been known from the seventeenth century, and had acquired simple motion (one slide over another) by 1736. From at latest 1826 there was a development of mechanical motion-picture devices, such as the wheelof-life, and these came to be linked with the magic lantern. The effect of persistence in human vision – that is to say, our capacity to hold the 'memory' of an image through an interval to the next image, thus allowing the possibility of a sequence built from rapidly succeeding units – had been known since classical times. Series of cameras photographing stages of a sequence were followed (Marey, 1882) by multiple-shot cameras. Friese-Greene and Edison worked on techniques of filming and projection, and celluloid was substituted for paper reels. By the 1890s the first public motion-picture shows were being given in France, America and England.

Television, as an idea, was involved with many of these developments. It is difficult to separate it, in its earliest stages, from photo-telegraphy. Bain proposed a device for transmitting pictures by electric wires in 1842; Bakewell in 1847 showed the copying telegraph; Caselli in 1862 transmitted pictures by wire over a considerable distance. In 1873, while working at a terminal of the Atlantic telegraph cable, May observed the light-sensitive properties of selenium (which had been isolated by Berzelius in 1817 and was in use for resistors). In a host of ways, following an already defined need, the means of transmitting still pictures and moving pictures were actively sought and to a considerable extent discovered. The list is long even when selective: Carey's electric eye in 1875; Nipkow's scanning system in 1884; Elster and Geitel's photoelectric cells in 1890; Braun's cathode-ray tube in 1897; Rosing's cathode-ray receiver in 1907; Campbell Swinton's electronic camera proposal in 1911. Through this whole period two facts are evident: that a system of television was foreseen, and its means were being actively sought; but also that, by comparison with electrical generation and electrical telegraphy and telephony, there was very little social investment to bring the scattered work together. It is true that there were technical blocks before 1914 – the thermionic valve and the multi-stage amplifier can be seen to have been needed and were not yet invented. But the critical difference between the various spheres of applied technology can be stated in terms of a social dimension: the new systems of production and of business or transport communication were already organised, at an economic level; the new systems of social communication were not. Thus when motion pictures were developed, their application was characteristically in the margin of established social forms – the sideshows – until their success was capitalised in a version of an established form, the motion-picture *theatre*.

The development of radio, in its significant scientific and technical stages between 1885 and 1911, was at first conceived, within already effective social systems, as an advanced form of telegraphy. Its application as a significantly new social form belongs to the immediate post-war period, in a changed social situation. It is significant that the hiatus in technical television development then also ended. In 1923 Zworykin introduced the electronic television camera tube. Through the early 1920s Baird and Jenkins, separately and competitively, were working on systems using mechanical scanning. From 1925 the rate of progress was qualitatively changed, through important technical advances but also with the example of sound broadcasting systems as a model. The Bell System in 1927 demonstrated wire transmission through a radio link, and the pre-history of the form can be seen to be ending. There was great rivalry between systems – especially those of mechanical and electronic scanning – and there is still great controversy about contributions and priorities. But this is characteristic of the phase in which the development of a technology moves into the stage of a new social form.

What is interesting throughout is that in a number of complex and related fields, these systems of mobility and transfer in production and communication, whether in mechanical and electric transport, or in telegraphy, photography, motion pictures, radio and television, were at once incentives and responses within a phase of general social transformation. Though some of the crucial scientific and technical discoveries were made by isolated and unsupported individuals, there was a crucial community of selected emphasis and intention, in a society characterised at its most general levels by a mobility and extension of the scale of organisations: forms of growth which brought with them immediate and longer-term problems of operative communication. In many different countries, and in apparently unconnected ways, such needs were at once isolated and technically defined. It is especially a characteristic of the communications systems that *all were foreseen – not in utopian but in technical ways – before the crucial components of the developed systems had been discovered and refined.* In no way is this a history of communications systems creating a new society or new social conditions. The decisive and earlier transformation of industrial production, and its new social forms, which had grown out of a long history of capital accumulation and working technical improvements, created new needs but also new possibilities, and the communications systems, down to television, were their intrinsic outcome.

C. THE SOCIAL HISTORY OF THE USES OF TELEVISION TECHNOLOGY

It is never quite true to say that in modern societies, when a social need has been demonstrated, its appropriate technology will be found. This is partly because some real needs, in any particular period, are beyond the scope of existing or foreseeable scientific and technical knowledge. It is even more because the key question, about technological response to a need, is less a question about the need itself than about its place in an existing social formation. A need which corresponds with the priorities of the real decision-making groups will, obviously, more quickly attract the investment of resources and the official permission, approval or encouragement on which a working technology, as distinct from available technical devices, depends. We can see this clearly in the major developments of industrial production and, significantly, in military technology. The social history of communications technology is interestingly different from either of these, and it is important to try to discover what are the real factors of this variation.

The problem must be seen at several different levels. In the very broadest perspective, there is an operative relationship between a new kind of expanded, mobile and complex society and the development of a modern communications technology. At one level this relationship can be reasonably seen as causal, in a direct way. The principal incentives to first-stage improvements in communications technology came from problems of communication and control in expanded military and commercial operations. This was both direct, arising from factors of greatly extending distance and scale, and indirect, as a factor within the development of transport technology, which was for obvious reasons the major direct response. Thus telegraphy and telephony, and in its early stages radio, were secondary factors within a primary communications system which was directly serving the needs of an established and developing military and commercial system. Through the nineteenth and into the twentieth century this was the decisive pattern.

But there were other social and political relationships and needs emerging from this complex of change. Indeed it is a consequence of the particular and dominant interpretation of these changes that the complex was at first seen as one requiring improvement in *operational* communication. The direct priorities of the expanding commercial system, and in certain periods of the military system, led to a definition of needs within the terms of these systems. The objectives and the consequent technologies were operational within the structures of these systems: passing necessary specific information, or maintaining contact and control. Modern electric technology, in this phase, was thus oriented to uses of person to person, operator and operative to operator and operative, within established specific structures. This quality can best be emphasised by contrast with the electric technology of the second phase, which was properly and significantly called *broadcasting*. A technology of specific messages to specific persons was complemented, but only relatively late, by a technology of varied messages to a general public.

Yet to understand this development we have to look at a wider communications system. The true basis of this system had preceded the developments in technology. Then as now there was a major, indeed dominant, area of social communication, by word of mouth, within every kind of social group. In addition, then as now, there were specific institutions of that kind of communication which involves or is predicated on social teaching and control: churches, schools, assemblies and proclamations, direction in places of work. All these interacted with forms of communication within the family.

What then were the new needs which led to the development of a new technology of social communication? The development of the press gives us the evidence for our first major instance. It was at once a response to the development of an extended social, economic and political system and a response to crisis within that system. The centralisation of political power led to a need for messages from that centre along other than official lines. Early newspapers were a combination of that kind of message – political and social information – and the specific messages – classified advertising and general commercial news – of an expanding system of trade. In Britain the development of the press went through its major formative stages in periods of crisis: the Civil War and Commonwealth, when the newspaper form was defined; the Industrial Revolution, when new forms of popular journalism were successively established; the major wars of the twentieth century, when the newspaper became a universal social form. For the transmission of simple orders, a communications system already existed. For the transmission of an ideology, there were specific traditional institutions. But for the transmission of news and background – the whole orienting, predictive and updating process which the fully developed press represented – there was an evident need for a new form, which the largely traditional institutions of church and school could not meet. And to the large extent that the crises of general change provoked both anxiety and controversy, this flexible and competitive form met social needs of a new kind. As the struggle for a share in decision and control became sharper, in campaigns for the vote and then in competition for the vote, the press became not only a new communications system but, centrally, a new social institution.

This can be interpreted as response to a political need and a political crisis, and it was certainly this. But a wider social need and social crisis can also be recognised. In a changing society, and especially after the Industrial Revolution, problems of social perspective and social orientation became more acute. New relations between men, and between men and things, were being intensely experienced, and in this area, especially, the traditional institutions of church and school, or of settled community and persisting family, had very little to say. A great deal was of course said, but from positions defined within an older kind of society. In a number of ways, and drawing on a range of impulses from curiosity to anxiety, new information and new kinds of orientation were deeply required: more deeply, indeed, than any specialisation to political, military or commercial information can account for. An increased awareness of mobility and change, not just as abstractions but as lived experiences, led to a major redefinition, in practice and then in theory, of the function and process of social communication.

What can be seen most evidently in the press can be seen also in the development of photography and the motion picture. The photograph is in one sense a popular extension of the portrait, for recognition and for record. But in a period of great mobility, with new separations of families and with internal and external migrations, it became more centrally necessary as a form of maintaining, over distance and through time, certain personal connections. Moreover, in altering relations to the physical world, the photograph as an object became a form of the photography of objects: moments of isolation and stasis within an experienced rush of change; and then, in its technical extension to motion, a means of observing and analysing motion itself, in new ways – a dynamic form in which new kinds of recognition were not only possible but necessary.

Now it is significant that until the period after the First World War, and in some ways until the period after the Second World War, these varying needs of a new kind of society and a new way of life were met by what were seen as specialised means: the press for political and economic information; the photograph for community, family and personal life; the motion picture for curiosity and entertainment; telegraphy and telephony for business information and some important personal messages. It was within this complex of specialised forms that broadcasting arrived.

The consequent difficulty of defining its social uses, and the intense kind of controversy which has ever since surrounded it, can then be more broadly understood. Moreover, the first definitions of broadcasting were made for sound radio. It is significant and perhaps puzzling that the definitions and institutions then created were those within which television developed.

We have now become used to a situation in which broadcasting is a major social institution, about which there is always controversy but which, in its familiar form, seems to have been predestined by the technology. This predestination, however, when closely examined, proves to be no more than a set of particular social decisions, in particular circumstances, which were then so widely if imperfectly ratified that it is now difficult to see them as decisions rather than as (retrospectively) inevitable results.

Thus, if seen only in hindsight, broadcasting can be diagnosed as a new and powerful form of social integration and control. Many of its main uses can be seen as socially, commercially and at times politically manipulative. Moreover, this viewpoint is rationalised by its description as 'mass communication', a phrase used by almost all its agents and advisers as well, curiously, as by most of its radical critics. 'Masses' had been the new nineteenth-century term of contempt for what was formerly described as 'the mob'. The physical 'massing' of the urban and industrial revolution underwrote this. A new radical class-consciousness adopted the term to express the material of new social formations: 'mass organisations'. The 'mass meeting' was an observable physical effect. So pervasive was this description that in the twentieth century multiple serial production was called, falsely but significantly, 'mass production': mass now meant large numbers (but within certain assumed social relationships) rather than any physical or social aggregate. Sound radio and television, for reasons we shall look at, were developed for transmission to *individual* homes, though there was nothing in the technology to make this inevitable. But then this new form of social communication – broadcasting – was obscured by its definition as 'mass communication': an abstraction to its most general characteristic, that it went to many people, 'the masses', which obscured the fact that the means chosen was the offer of individual sets, a method much better described by the earlier word 'broadcasting'. It is interesting that the only developed 'mass' use of radio was in Nazi Germany, where under Goebbels' orders the Party organised compulsory public listening groups and the receivers were in the streets. There has been some imitation of this by similar regimes, and Goebbels was deeply interested in television for the same kind of use. What was developed within most capitalist societies, though called 'mass communication', was significantly different.

There was early official intervention in the development of broadcasting, but in form this was only at a technical level. In the earlier struggle against the development of the press, the State had licensed and taxed newspapers, but for a century before the coming of broadcasting the alternative idea of an independent press had been realised both in practice and in theory. State intervention in broadcasting had some real and some plausible technical grounds: the distribution of wavelengths. But to these were added, though always controversially, more general social directions or attempts at direction. This social history of broadcasting can be discussed on its own, at the levels of practice and principle. Yet it is unrealistic to extract it from another and perhaps more decisive process, through which in particular economic situations, a set of scattered technical devices became an applied technology and then a social technology.

A Fascist regime might quickly see the use of broadcasting for direct political and social control. But that, in any case, was when the technology had already been developed elsewhere. In capitalist democracies, the thrust for conversion from scattered techniques to a technology was not political but economic. The characteristically isolated inventors, from Nipkow and Rosing to Baird and Jenkins and Zwyorkin, found their point of development, if at all, in the manufacturers and prospective manufacturers of the technical apparatus. The history at one level is of these isolated names, but at another level it is of EMI, RCA and a score of similar companies and corporations. In the history of motion pictures, capitalist development was primarily in production; large-scale capitalist distribution came much later, as a way of controlling and organising a market for given production. In broadcasting, both in sound radio and later in television, the major investment was in the means of distribution, and was devoted to production only so far as to make the distribution technically possible and then attractive. Unlike all previous communications technologies, radio and television were *systems primarily devised for transmission and reception as abstract processes, with little or no definition of preceding content*. When the question of content was raised, it was resolved, in the main, parasitically. There were state occasions, public sporting events, theatres and so on, which would be communicatively distributed by these new technical means. *It is not only that the supply of broadcasting facilities preceded the demand; it is that the means of communication preceded their content.*

The period of decisive development in sound broadcasting was the 1920s. After the technical advances in sound telegraphy which had been made for military purposes during the war, there was at once an economic opportunity and the need for a new social definition. No nation or manufacturing group held a monopoly of the technical means of broadcasting, and there was a period of intensive litigation followed by cross-licensing of the scattered basic components of successful transmission and reception (the vacuum tube or valve, developed from 1904 to 1913; the feedback circuit, developed from 1912; the neutrodyne and heterodyne circuits, from 1923). Crucially, in the mid-1920s, there was a series of investment-guided technical solutions to the problem of building a small and simple domestic receiver, on which the whole qualitative transformation from wireless telegraphy to broadcasting depended. By the mid-1920s – 1923 and 1924 are especially decisive years – this breakthrough had happened in the leading industrial societies: the United States, Britain, Germany and France. By the end of the 1920s the radio industry had become a major sector of industrial production, within a rapid general expansion of the new kinds of machines which were eventually to be called 'consumer durables'. This complex of developments included the motorcycle and motor-car, the box camera and its successors, home electrical appli-ances, and radio sets. Socially, this complex is characterised by the two apparently paradoxical yet deeply connected tendencies of modern urban industrial living: on the one hand mobility, on the other hand the more apparently self-sufficient family home. The earlier period of public technology, best exemplified by the railways and city lighting, was being replaced by a kind of technology for which no satisfactory name has yet been found: that which served an at once mobile and home-centred way of living: a form of *mobile privatisation*. Broadcasting in its applied form was a social product of this distinctive tendency.

The contradictory pressures of this phase of industrial capitalist society were indeed resolved, at a certain level, by the institution of broadcasting. For mobility was only in part the impulse of an independent curiosity: the wish to go out and see new places. It was essentially an impulse formed in the break-down and dissolution of older and smaller kinds of settlement and productive labour. The new and larger settlements and industrial organisations required major internal mobility, at a primary level, and this was joined by secondary consequences in the dispersal of extended families and in the needs of new kinds of social organisation. Social processes long implicit in the revolution of industrial capitalism were then greatly intensified: especially an increasing distance between immediate living areas and the directed places of work and government. No effective kinds of social control over these transformed industrial and political processes had come anywhere near being achieved or even foreseen. Most people were living in the fall-out area of processes determined beyond them. What had been gained, nevertheless, in intense social struggle, had been the improvement of immediate conditions, within the limits and pressures of these decisive large-scale processes. There was some relative improvement in wages and working conditions, and there was a qualitative change in the distribution of the day, the week and the year between work and off-work periods. These two effects combined in a major emphasis on improvement of the small family home. Yet this privatisation, which was at once an effective achievement and a defensive response, carried, as a consequence, an imperative need for new kinds of contact. The new homes might appear private and 'self-sufficient' but could be maintained only by regular funding and supply from external sources, and these, over a range from employment and prices to depressions and wars, had a decisive and often a disrupting influence on what was nevertheless seen as a separable 'family' project. This relationship created both the need and the form of a new kind of 'communication': news from 'outside', from otherwise inaccessible sources. Already in the drama of the 1880s and 1890s (Ibsen, Chekhov) this structure had appeared: the centre of dramatic interest was now for the first time the family home, but men and women stared from its windows, or waited anxiously for messages, to learn about forces, 'out there', which would determine the conditions of their lives. The new 'consumer' technology which reached its first decisive stage in the 1920s served this complex of needs within just these limits and pressures. There were immediate improvements of the condition and efficiency of the privatised home; there were new facilities, in private transport, for expeditions from the home; and then, in radio, there was a facility for a new kind of social input – news and entertainment brought into the home. Some people spoke of the new machines as gadgets, but they were always much more than this. They were the applied technology of a set of emphases and responses within the determining limits and pressures of industrial capitalist society.

The cheap radio receiver is then a significant index of a general condition and response. It was especially welcomed by all those who had least social opportunities of other kinds; who lacked independent mobility or access to the previously diverse places of entertainment and information. Broadcasting could also come to serve, or seem to serve, as a form of *unified* social intake, at the most general levels. What had been intensively promoted by the radio manufacturing companies thus interlocked with this kind of social need, itself defined within general limits and pressures. In the early stages of radio manufacturing, transmission was conceived before content. By the end of the 1920s the network was there, but still at a low level of content-definition. It was in the 1930s, in the second phase of radio, that most of the significant advances in content were made. The transmission and reception networks created, *as a by-product*, the facilities of primary broadcasting production. But the general social definition of 'content' was already there.

This theoretical model of the general development of broadcasting is necessary to an understanding of the particular development of television. For there were, in the abstract, several different ways in which television as a technical means might have been developed. After a generation of universal domestic television it is not easy to realise this. But it remains true that, after a great deal of intensive research and development, the domestic television set is in a number of ways an inefficient medium of visual broadcasting. Its visual inefficiency by comparison with the cinema is especially striking, whereas in the case of radio there was by the 1930s a highly efficient sound broadcasting receiver, without any real competitors in its own line. Within the limits of the television home-set emphasis it has so far not been possible to make more than minor qualitative improvements. Higher-definition systems, and colour, have still only brought the domestic television set, as a machine, to the standard of a very inferior kind of cinema. Yet most people have adapted to this inferior visual medium, in an unusual kind of preference for an inferior immediate technology, because of the social complex – and especially that of the privatised home – within which broadcasting, as a system, is operative. The cinema had remained at an earlier level of social definition; it was and remains a special kind of theatre, offering specific and discrete works of one general kind. Broadcasting, by contrast, offered a whole social intake: music, news, entertainment, sport. The advantages of this general intake, within the home, much more than outweighed the technical advantages of visual transmission and reception in the cinema, confined as this was to specific and discrete works. While broadcasting was confined to sound, the powerful visual medium of cinema was an immensely popular alternative. But when broadcasting became visual, the option for its social advantages outweighed the immediate technical deficits.

The transition to television broadcasting would have occurred quite generally in the late 1930s and early 1940s, if the war had not intervened. Public television services had begun in Britain in 1936 and in the United States in 1939, but with still very expensive receivers. The full investment in transmission and reception facilities did not occur until the late 1940s and early 1950s, but the growth was thereafter very rapid. The key social tendencies which had led to the definition of broadcasting were by then even more pronounced. There was significantly higher investment in the privatised home, and the social and physical distances between these homes and the decisive political and productive centres of the society had become much greater. Broadcasting, as it had developed in radio, seemed an inevitable model: the central transmitters and the domestic sets.

Television then went through some of the same phases as radio. Essentially, again, the technology of transmission and reception developed before the content, and important parts of the content were and have remained by-products of the technology rather than independent enterprises. As late as the introduction of colour, 'colourful' programmes were being devised to persuade people to buy colour sets. In the earliest stages there was the familiar parasitism on existing events: a coronation, a major sporting event, theatres. A comparable parasitism on the cinema was slower to show itself, until the decline of the cinema altered the terms of trade; it is now very widespread, most evidently in the United States. But again, as in radio, the end of the first general decade brought significant independent television production. By the middle and late 1950s, as in radio in the middle and late 1930s, new kinds of programme were being made for television and there were very important advances in the productive use of the medium, including, as again at a comparable stage in radio, some kinds of original work.

Yet the complex social and technical definition of broadcasting led to inevitable difficulties, especially in the productive field. What television could do relatively cheaply was to transmit something that was in any case happening or had happened. In news, sport, and some similar areas it could provide a service of transmission at comparatively low cost. But in every kind of new work, which it had to produce, it became a very expensive medium, within the broadcasting model. It was never as expensive as film, but the cinema, as a distributive medium, could directly control its revenues. It was, on the other hand, implicit in broadcasting that given the tunable receiver all programmes could be received without immediate charge. There could have been and can still be a socially financed system of production and distribution within which local and specific charges would be unnecessary; the BBC, based on the licence system for domestic receivers, came nearest to this. But short of monopoly, which still exists in some state-controlled systems, the problems of investment for production, in any broadcasting system, are severe.

Thus within the broadcasting model there was this deep contradiction, of centralised transmission and privatised reception. One economic response was licensing. Another, less direct, was commercial sponsorship and then supportive advertising. But the crisis of production control and financing has been endemic in broadcasting precisely because of the social and technical model that was adopted and that has become so deeply established. The problem is masked, rather than solved, by the fact that as a transmitting technology – its functions largely limited to relay and commentary on other events – some balance could be struck; a limited revenue could finance this limited service. But many of the creative possibilities of television have been frustrated precisely by this apparent solution, and this has far more than local effects on producers and on the balance of programmes. When there has been such heavy investment in a particular model of social communications, there is a restraining complex of financial institutions, of cultural expectations and of specific technical developments, which though it can be seen, superficially, as the effect of a technology is in fact a social complex of a new and central kind.

It is against this background that we have to look at the development of broadcasting institutions, at their uses of the media, and at the social problems of the new technical phase which we are about to enter.

2. Institutions of the technology

The technology of broadcasting was introduced as a marginal element in very complex social structures. It is indeed difficult to realise how marginal it then seemed, as we look back from a period in which broadcasting policies have become a central issue of politics. The key factor in the earlier period, as has already been emphasised, was that the directing impulse came from the manufacturers of broadcasting apparatus, and especially of receivers. Yet because of the general importance of radio telephony there was always another kind of pressure, from political authorities: questions of the security and integrity of the nation-state were implicitly and at times explicitly raised, but were complicated by the fact that the political authorities were thinking primarily of radio telephony while the manufacturers were looking forward to broadcasting. In Britain all transmitters and receivers had to be licensed by the Post Office, under an Act dating from 1904. When the Marconi company began broadcasting in 1920, there were complaints that this use for entertainment of what was primarily a commercial and transport-control medium was frivolous and dangerous, and there was even a temporary ban, under pressure from radio-telephonic interests and the Armed Forces. There were then complicated negotiations between the competing manufacturers, the Post Office and the Armed Services Committee; and in 1922 a consortium of manufacturers, who would provide programmes under terms agreed with the Post Office and the Government, was formed as the British Broadcasting Company. The keys to this agreement were the granting of monopoly to the Company and the decision to finance broadcasting by the sale of licences for receivers. In the period 1925–1926, through continuous controversy and negotiation, what had been essentially a public utility company was becoming a true public broadcasting corporation: the BBC which received its charter in 1926. Granted the elements of monopoly and of guaranteed finance from the sale of licences, it acquired as a by-product of regulation the necessary continuity and resources to become a producer rather than merely a transmitter of broadcasting. This qualitative change in the character of the institution was never clearly foreseen, at least by a majority of those involved in the negotiations, and its potential would not have been realised if the definition of broadcasting as a public service – which at the time meant very different things – had not been specialised, by its early controllers, to a positive programming policy. The specific elements in the British solution can be seen as threefold:

(i) the early development of Britain as an industrial society, with an extended communications network over a relatively small geographical area, had already to an important extent 'nationalised' its culture; it had, for example, led to a predominantly national press.

(ii) a dominant version of the national culture had already been established, in an unusually compact ruling-class, so that public service could be effectively understood and administered as service according to the values of an existing public definition, with an effective paternalist definition of both service and responsibility.

(iii) the character of the British State which, because of the compactness of its ruling-class, proceeded in many matters by appointment and delegation rather than by centralised state administration. This permitted the emergence of a state-regulated and state-sponsored public corporation which was yet not subject to detailed state control. The flexibility which was latent in this kind of

solution, though continually a matter of dispute, permitted the emergence of an independent corporate broadcasting policy, in which the independence was at once
real, especially in relation to political parties and temporary administrations, and qualified, by its definition in
terms of a pre-existing cultural hegemony.

These were specific factors within what is otherwise a common
area of pressures, as broadcasting was developed not only
within a capitalist society but specifically by the capitalist manufacturers of the technological apparatus. As the varying solutions
in different capitalist societies are examined it is clear that the
technology as such was in no way determining. The bargain
struck in Britain between state and capitalist interests was in
terms of a limited separation of powers. The more typical
solution, in Western European societies of a similar size, was
direct state regulation of broadcasting, at the level of its early
technical regulation, leading to direct state regulation of broadcasting production, as still for example in Italy and France. In
Fascist societies this direct state control was a natural instrument
of policy. In communist societies state control of broadcasting
was rationalised as the guarantee and instrument of popular
power.

The alternative solution, in a quite different direction, was
that established in the United States. There was always pressure
to control broadcasting in the national interest, but the manufacturers of equipment were too powerful to be controlled, and
the competing consortia which they formed pushed out directly
into a rapidly expanding market. Federal control was only
established after the technical consequences of this kind of
expansion had become chaotic, at that level of technology. The
early broadcasting networks were federations of prime manufacturers, who then acquired production facilities as an essentially secondary operation: secondary, that is, to the production
and selling of sets. The finance for production, in this highly
competitive situation, was drawn from advertising, in its two
forms of insertion and sponsorship. More clearly than anywhere

else, because all countervailing factors were less strong, the American institutions realised the pure forms of a simple applied technology. The manufacturing institutions, both directly in the sale of sets and indirectly in the supply of advertising money, determined the shape of broadcasting institutions. Thus the broadcasting public was effectively, from the beginning, the competitive broadcasting market. The major networks, which began forming in 1926, became the characteristic institutions of both radio and eventually television. Public service in any other than a market sense developed within a structure already dominated by these institutions. As it eventually emerged it was a classic kind of market-regulatory control, into which were inserted, always with difficulty and controversy, notions of a non-market public interest. Until 1927 the market competition was open and direct. From 1927 to 1932 the new Federal Radio Commission organised a system of allocation of frequencies, and from 1932 to 1937 attempted to control specific abuses, such as fraud. The 'airways', it was decided, were public property, and licence was given to competitors to use them, under technical controls and then regulatory controls to prevent specific abuses. From 1937, in radio and in the early period of television, the FRC, now the Federal Communications Commission, tried to keep the competitive market open, against strong tendencies to monopoly, especially in production. It was mainly after 1944 that the FCC began to try to define the public interest in terms other than keeping the market open. It sought to introduce standards of social usefulness, of political fairness, and of public morality. In the period of the development of television, these attempts were redoubled, but the structure of the existing institutions led to curious anomalies. Thus the Commission could revoke a station's licence, but could not really control the networks to which some of the stations belonged and others were affiliated. For most programme production, the networks were obviously responsible, yet the effective controls were on stations. This anomaly has worked both ways. A political administration seeking to control or limit television freedom (as under Nixon in 1972–73) can try to use pressure on the indivi-

dual stations to get them to put pressures on the networks; mainly
to alter their political content, especially in news reporting and
commentary. This is rationalised as 'community control' of the
'irresponsible' networks, and the networks are indeed large
private corporations without public responsibility. Yet since the
stations are bought and sold, subject to licence, they are themselves a capitalist version of community interests, but a small-
scale capitalism dependent on the large-scale networks for
broadcast production of any fully developed kind. Much of the
argument about 'community television', in other societies, shows
the same features of uneven competition between monopoly or
network interests, small-scale local or pseudo-local capitalism,
and the political power of the state.

It is then possible to abstract the basic early development of
television institutions as a contrast or competition between
'public service' and 'commercial' institutions. In Britain, especially, this has seemed a natural perspective, since the unique
'public service' definition of the BBC was in the mid-1950s
successfully challenged by, and made competitive with, a commercial network: the Independent Television Authority (now
the Independent Broadcasting Authority, with the addition of
commercial local radio stations). This public authority (public
in legal status and in the character of its constitution, commercial
in its dependence for income on its contracted companies) owns
its means of transmission but contracts for the provision of
programmes with a number of regional companies. These
obtain their own funds from selling insertion-advertisement
time, and a national network and programming, dominated by
the larger companies from the richer regions, is then built up,
with some local variations. This network has been, from the
beginning, of a commercial type, with a built-in relationship
between 'peak-hour' programme planning and the selling of
advertising time. In this sense, the contrast between 'public
service' and 'commercial' television holds good, and in programming this is significant (as will be seen in Chapter 4,
below).

The same kind of contrast, though in more limited terms, can be made in the United States, where the first development was commercial and a public-service element was later added, in the margin or as a palliative. The Public Broadcasting Corporation was established as late as 1967, building on earlier work of the National Educational Television organisation (from 1952) and the Public Broadcasting Laboratory. Local stations of this type had been established from the 1950s (e.g. KQED, San Francisco, 1954), and there were Federal grants for station combination and co-operation from 1962. Throughout its development, this public-service television has been a poor relation of the commercial networks. Its production funds are subject to central control and in fact, through this, to political decision. The stations themselves are member-supported, and survive with great difficulty only by constant local fund-raising. Once again, however, the 'public service' and 'commercial' contrast has not only an institutional but a programming significance (see below, Chapter 4).

So useful a perspective ought not to be given up lightly. Yet it has to be critically reviewed in two respects: first, to take account of the ordinary terms of the commercial broadcasters' offensive against it; second, and more important, to take account of the complicated relationship between a public authority and state and corporate political and economic interests.

As in the general rhetoric of the defence of capitalism, commercial broadcasting does not call itself commercial, let alone capitalist. It uses public-relations descriptions like 'free' and 'independent', and often contrasts itself with 'monopoly' and 'state control'. This rhetoric dissolves when we look at the character of the large American broadcasting corporations or of the British programme companies. In different ways these are conglomerates of established capital interests. (The difference between them follows from the earlier history of the institutions, in that the American corporations belong to the large-capital spectrum, while the British companies are mainly in the medium and even small-capital range.) Whatever public controls or policy definitions may then be set, the institutions have as their primary aim the realisation and distribution of private profit on invested capital, and this visibly affects their major policies. By contrast the public-service institutions are in effect non-profit-making, so that revenue is devoted almost wholly to production and development of the broadcasting service. Up to this point the contrast still holds, and needs to be emphasised.

Yet there is, at the next level, an undoubted ambiguity about the public interest, and especially about its relation to the State. Here a liberal rhetoric can be equally confusing, for there is no simple equation between the State in a capitalist society and the public interest in its broadest definition. The point is made harder to see by the existence of true state monopolies in broadcasting, as in societies modelled on the Soviet Union and as in some West European and developing countries. Here the state can be correctly identified with a partisan version of the public interest (whether approved or not, by those subject to it and by observers, is another question) and state control of broadcasting is a function of general state control of information and ideology. Where competitive versions of the public interest have in effect been eliminated, the situation is simple, if also dead. But where such competitive versions are active, as for example in France and Italy, the equation between state and public interest is especially vulnerable, and this leads not only to internal conflicts but, in modern conditions, to complicated international pressures which we shall have to examine. In the United States, where it was federal action, in response to many public and local initiatives, which established a limited public-service network, there is as yet no sign of any real insulation of a continuing broad-term public interest from the temporary political pressures of particular administrations. But even where such an insulation exists, as to some extent genuinely in Britain, in the case of the BBC, the equation of state and public interest, at the level of the formula of the public corporation or authority, must not be uncritically accepted. In real terms, after all, the government appoints the public authorities: characteristically, in Britain, former Ministers and politicians and members of the available full-time and part-time administrative bureaucracy. It is done with some skill and with the kind of window-dressing of marginal appointments on which any such system depends for its apparent legitimacy. But within its conventional terms all proposals for directly elected authorities, or for measures of internal democratic representation or control by actual producers and broadcasters, are very vigorously opposed. The authorities, as they stand, are then part of a complicated patronage system on which the real state, as distinct from the formal state, effectively relies. It is much less rigid than formal control through a Ministry, and it allows for marginal controversy between the competitive political parties. In the looseness and indefinition of some of its structures it further allows for some genuine independence from immediate and short-term government pressures. But it depends, finally, on a consensus version of the 'public' or 'national' interest: a consensus which is first assumed and then vigorously practised, rather than a consensus which has ever been openly arrived at and made subject to regular open review.

Moreover, in all these varying systems the terms of the discussion of broadcasting institutions have remained obstinately local and marginal, while the real situation has become very general and highly dynamic. Essentially, the mode of discussion of broadcasting institutions has remained in what can best be called a pre-1950s stage, while the developments of the 1950s and after have opened up a quite different broadcasting world.

B. TYPES OF CURRENT DEVELOPMENT

In the whole non-communist world the determining factor in broadcasting development, since the 1950s, has been the expansion of the American communications system. This has to be understood in two related stages: the formation, in the United States, of a complex military, political and industrial communications system; and then, in direct relation to this, the operation of this system to penetrate the broadcasting systems of all other available states.[1]

There has been a close relation in the United States, since the

[1] I am especially indebted in this section to Herbert I. Schiller: *Mass Communications and American Empire*: Kelley, New York, 1970.

Second World War, between military and political communications research and development, and what is still thought of in a separate way as general broadcasting. There has been continual interaction between governmental investment in new communications and electronic techniques and the general development of broadcasting facilities: the case of television satellite broadcasting (to be examined in detail in Chapter 6, below) is only the most spectacular. During the 1950s and 1960s the institutional framework of broadcasting became very complicated, with an uncertain frontier between military and political and general institutions. Thus the Interdepartment Radio Advisory Committee, concerned with the allocation of frequencies, moved from civilian to military control, and this emphasis was extended into international negotiations. In the early 1960s a National Communications System, with a directorate of telecommunications, was established for direct governmental purposes, but had some effect on the development of general broadcasting. The overlap of procurement between state and network agencies, and the ties between general electronic and broadcasting corporations (e.g. the Radio Corporation of America which is an electronics manufacturer as well as the owner of one of the three main networks, the National Broadcasting Corporation), led to a situation in which it was not possible to separate, into distinct categories, military electronics, government agencies concerned with information and propaganda, and the most visible institutions of general 'commercial' broadcasting. From this it was only a short but deliberate step to the operation of this network on an international scale, over a range from space communications and communication satellites to the planned export of propaganda, information and entertainment broadcasting. Thus the Department of Defence has a world-wide network of 38 television and over 200 radio transmitters, and the great majority of its audience is non-American. The United States Information Agency has transmitters and prepares programmes for use in foreign countries: many of these programmes are not identified, when shown on foreign American-controlled or American-sponsored stations, as USIAoriginated. In quantity this direct governmental intervention beyond its frontiers is overshadowed by the dynamic export policies of the broadcasting corporations, over a range from equipment and management to programme sales. In more than ninety foreign countries, the three leading corporations have subsidiaries, stations and networking contracts; they are particularly strong in Latin America, the Caribbean, Africa, Asia and the Middle East. From this base there is continual pressure, some of it already successful, to penetrate societies with developed broadcasting systems, in which various forms of local governmental control have prevented ordinary expansion. This pressure has included arrangements with local groups seeking commercial broadcasting, often requiring a change of national law. In a number of cases, including some planned 'pirate' broadcasting – often represented in local terms as a few small independent operators against the local state monopoly – the planning and finance have come from the United States. Much of this penetration is seen only in terms of the sale of programmes, which is indeed important, representing the difference between profit and loss for all U.S. telefilm production, and already, in some countries, accounting for a significant and in some cases a major part of all television programming. But the expansion has to be seen also as serving the international advertiser, for in a trading world dominated by para-national companies and U.S. subsidiaries the provision of programmes and types of service which open the way to international commercial advertising has this inevitable perspective. The 'commercial' character of television has then to be seen at several levels: as the making of programmes for profit in a known market; as a channel for advertising; and as a cultural and political form directly shaped by and dependent on the norms of a capitalist society, selling both consumer goods and a 'way of life' based on them, in an ethos that is at once locally generated, by domestic capitalist interests and authorities, and internationally organised, as a political project, by the dominant capitalist power. It is then not too much to say that the general transition, in the last twenty years, from what was normally a national and state-controlled sound broadcasting to what are now, in world terms, predominantly commercial television institutions, is a consequence of this planned operation from the United States. What surfaces in one country after another as a local argument, and is quickly and persuasively described as a choice between 'state monopoly' and 'independent broadcasting', is in the overwhelming majority of cases a put-up job by these American interests, their local associates, and the powerful international advertising companies.

The terms of the older argument about broadcasting institutions are then not only inadequate but sometimes positively misleading. In the developing world old films and television programmes are in effect dumped, at prices which make any local production seem ludicrously expensive by comparison. A market is then created in which available entertainment, advertising and general political and cultural influence come in a single 'cheap' package. In developed countries, including those in which primary television production is at a higher level than in the United States itself, the graded export price is still favourably competitive with primary national production, and the degree of dependence on advertising revenue, within a broadcasting institution, tends to settle how far the door will be opened to this kind of commercial penetration. Where any particular nation holds out there are internal campaigns for a change of policy, in which local branches of the international advertising agencies are heavily involved, and, as has been noted, there are planned frontier stations and pirate transmitters, aiming to 'capture' domestic audiences. Even in Britain, where another tradition was strong, the campaigns to commercialise both television and radio have eventually succeeded, at least in part. In many other countries, and especially in small- and medium-scale societies which find a primary-producing television service expensive, the effective penetration is now virtually complete.

It is then in this precise context that new and very powerful technical means are being introduced: especially satellite television transmission. It is clear that in some societies, with established national traditions and institutions in modern broad-casting, certain controls against the global commercialisation of television have some chance of success. But throughout the monopoly-capitalist period of communications institutions it has been evident that the level of viability, the scale-mark of inde-pendent survival, rises continuously, and at times dramatically, as the general market is extended. Just as a nineteenth-century popular newspaper, in Britain, could survive and flourish with a circulation of 100,000, but is now in danger at anything less than 2,000,000, so a television service, in conditions of un-controlled and therefore unequal competition, may pass very quickly from healthy viability to chronic financial crisis. It may then, if nothing else is done, either surrender to the general trend or, more subtly, change itself internally to survive within the trend: a change which will have its clear origins in the general pressures but which will usually be rationalised as some form of independent 'modernisation'.

I shall return to these questions about institutions, especially as they relate to the new and emerging technologies, in Chapter 6. Meanwhile, to regain the substance of the medium, we need to look more closely at television as a cultural form.

3. The forms of television

There is a complicated interaction between the technology of television and the received forms of other kinds of cultural and social activity. Many people have said that television is essentially a combination and development of earlier forms: the newspaper, the public meeting, the educational class, the theatre, the cinema, the sports stadium, the advertising columns and billboards. The development is complicated in some cases by the earlier precedents of radio, and these will need to be considered. Yet it is clearly not only a question of combination and development. The adaptation of received forms to the new technology has led in a number of cases to significant changes and to some real qualitative differences. It is worth looking at each of the main forms with these questions in mind. But when we have done this, it will be necessary also to look at those forms which are not in any obvious way derivative, and which can usefully be seen as the innovating forms of television itself.

A. COMBINATION AND DEVELOPMENT OF EARLIER FORMS

(i) *News*

The newspaper had gone through all its major phases of development before the coming of broadcast news. In the early days of radio there was virtually absolute dependence on existing press agencies for the collection of news. Techniques of broadcast presentation were at first the simple transmission of news agency dispatches read by 'announcers' who were assumed to be at once authoritative and neutral, though the real 'authority' and 'neutrality' were those of the agencies. The use of special broadcasting reporters and correspondents developed mainly during the Second World War. By the time a majority television service was being developed, there were specific internal facilities for news gathering and news presentation, although the general news agencies continued to be used.

Relations between the broadcast news bulletin and the newspaper, as forms, are then complicated. They can best be analysed under four headings: sequence; priority; personal presentation; visualisation.

(a) Sequence

The printed page of the ordinary newspaper had become, before television, a mosaic of items. Earlier newspapers had followed a certain sequence, by column division. But even before this division had been broken down to the mosaic layout which was common in most papers from the 1920s, the act of reading a newspaper page involved a glancing over or scanning, and then, within the terms of the newspaper's selection, the reader's selection of items on which to concentrate. Since particular pages of the paper were specialised to certain kinds of news and related material, any particular mosaic page was then itself selected, before scanning within the mosaic began.

Some elements of this virtually simultaneous presentation of a number of news items were technically possible in broadcasting, and have to a limited extent been used. But the simplest mode of presentation in broadcasting was linear in time. In British radio it was only during the war that what were still called, from newspaper practice, 'headlines' were assembled at the beginning of the bulletin. This kind of headlining is now widely used in television newscasts, although not universally. Repetition of the main points at the end of the bulletin is again common but not universal. Yet whether or not these techniques of attention and repetition are locally employed, the main form of television news is, within its own structure, linear.

(b) Priorities

Linear presentation has necessary effects on questions of priority between news items. The mosaic newspaper page has its own techniques of catching attention and indicating relative importance, but these are to a certain extent subject to the reader's capacity to find his own way through. The broadcast news bulletin thus tends to retain more apparent editorial control of priority and attention.

It is impossible to estimate the effects of this without looking at what had happened to priorities in different kinds of newspaper. In Britain, for example, a comparison of lead stories (see *Communications*, 1966, pp. 76–82) showed marked variations of priorities in different kinds of paper. A further comparison with broadcast bulletins showed that broadcasting priorities were, on the whole, those of the minority press. In the United States the press situation is different, but the general point still holds. The world-view indicated by the selection and relative priority of news items is very similar as between broadcast bulletins and those minority newspapers which are written by and for the relatively highly educated. The distribution of interests in the more popular press, which supposedly follows the interests of its characteristic readers, is hardly to be found anywhere in broadcast news, although very similar definitions of what is popular and interesting tend to predominate in the non-news programming.

The effects of this are complex. It can be said that the broadcast bulletins impose certain priorities, and that among these are characteristic definitions of high politics, with a centralising emphasis on the acts and words of political leaders. Yet, though this is in general true, the national television news bulletins provide more public news than all but a very few newspapers. Moreover, they provide this to a very wide public, in ways that would not happen if we had only a 'minority' and a 'popular' press.

(c) Presentation

In Britain until the Second World War, the broadcast announcer was an anonymous authoritative (ruling-class) voice. Personal identification was introduced only as a security measure under the threat of invasion and capture of the stations. In television personal identification has become more marked, though in BBC bulletins it is still only lightly emphasised, while in ITN bulletins the formula is 'the news with . . .' and then the names of the readers. This is also a common formula in American newscasts, but then there is additionally, as in most American television, immediate self-introduction.

Through any of these formulas the visual presence of a familiar presenter is bound to affect the whole communication situation. The BBC, at one extreme, tries continually to limit the presenter to a reading function, going out of its way to show him being handed papers or with the news-writers visible behind him. At the other extreme, in the mixed bulletins of local and national and international news in American television, there is a studied informality which is meant to create the effect of a group of men telling you things they happen to know. Even in the network bulletins there is less emphasis on a script and more on a personal presentation. Further, in the network bulletins, one of the presenters normally ends with a commentary, of an editorial kind, including relatively controversial points. In BBC television, commentary is strictly separated from the presenter, and specialist 'correspondents' are introduced to give what is in effect – though local neutrality is usually maintained – an editorial interpretation or point of view.

Most television news now includes a large number of reports from outside the studio, by reporters on the spot or in the wings. There is a variation of formula here also. In BBC bulletins it is 'our reporter' but it is 'his report'. In many American bulletins there is a closer identification between the central presentation and the substance of the distant report. This difference is quite marked in matters of commentary and interpretation, which at least formally, in BBC bulletins, are placed as the views of a section editor or correspondent. Though these differences are quite important, most of them are in practice overridden by the generalised authority of the presentation as a whole.

(d) Visualisation

Much of the real content of news has been altered by the facts of visual presentation. In certain kinds of report there seems to be an absolute difference between the written or spoken account and the visual record with commentary. It is true that much can be altered by selection and editing, but of course this is true also of any observer's account. It can be reasonably argued that the televisual impression of 'seeing the events for oneself' is at times and perhaps always deceptive. It matters very much, for example, in the visual reporting of a civil disturbance, whether 'the camera' is looking over the heads of the police being stoned or over the heads of the demonstrators being tear-gassed. The former is much more common, and the 'middle' view, which is often attempted in commentary, is rarely visually present – a fact which can make the 'neutrality' of the commentary essentially abstract. An intermediary is always present if not visible, and this can be more misleading than situations in which awareness of an intermediary is inevitable. Such awareness, however, is commonly absorbed, to an important degree, by habituation and routine, and indeed there are many events which come through the television camera with less processing or filtration than in any other medium. This has had important effects in the reporting of wars, natural disasters and famines. Its effect has also been important in the matter of political leaders, who are now less protected by standard communication formulas such as 'the President said . . .', and who, in spite of many consequent devices, are more regularly visible as whole persons. This has had complicated and controversial effects on many of the styles of politics. However, when we add the general facts of visualisation to the altered selections and priorities of the broadcast bulletins, we have to see a qualitative difference, and almost certainly a qualitative gain, in television as compared with printed news. Print, of course, retains its incomparable advantages as a way of collecting, recalling and checking information.

One significant difference between current British and American television should be noted in this context. British news bulletins now make much more intensive use of visual material beyond the immediate presentation. Indeed it is sometimes possible to feel, in British bulletins, that the item is there, or has that priority, because the film has come in. Or, if the film is not available, still photographs of people and events in the news fill the whole screen while much of the report is being read. In American bulletins, by contrast, the most obvious opportunities for this kind of visualisation – whether by film or stills – are often as it were deliberately ignored. The main visual experience of an American news bulletin is of the news readers themselves, with very simple visual background signs, and in current practice a significantly lower proportion of filmed reports, especially in regional news. Accustomed to British television news presentation, I felt after watching some weeks of American television bulletins that some new term was needed: perhaps 'visual radio'. I do not know all the reasons for this difference. There are some obvious problems of physical distance. But in regional and local bulletins many obvious opportunities for visual presentation are not taken. It presumably makes the news service very much cheaper to run. On the other hand, where there has been good visual reporting, as in some of the powerful film from Vietnam, the effect is proportionately very much more striking.

(ii) *Argument and Discussion*

There can be little doubt that broadcasting as a whole, and television especially, has markedly broadened the forms of public argument and discussion. All earlier forms, in large-scale societies, were more limited in character and scale. The sermon, the lecture, the political address were obviously more limited in immediate points of view. Only in certain favourable situations was there that regular choice and variety of viewpoints which is now common within even the limited range of current television argument. Public debates and meetings, or sessions of local and national government, reached many fewer people. Only a few newspapers, and some minority magazines, opened their columns to a wide range of controversy.

Yet it has been difficult to acknowledge this qualitative change because of the various restrictions still placed on the full range of argument. In some services there is a regular and virtually absolute exclusion of oppositional or minority views. When there is any change in this, as in Prague with Dubcek, the extent of the repression but also of the consequent potential for liberation can be seen as remarkable. It is then useful to compare the situation in relatively open societies such as Britain and the United States. At first glance, American television is much more open to public argument. There is a crucial difference in the fact that many public proceedings in the United States, from Senate hearings to local schools boards, are broadcast or televised, whereas in Britain there have been repeated refusals to allow the televising or broadcasting of any parliamentary proceedings. Again, there is the American use of the 'free speech message', which usually comes among the commercials. This excludes certain categories of message which are subject to law or formal vote, but includes points of view about a wide range of public actions and attitudes, given on the speaker's own responsibility. Again, there is rather more public questioning of local elected officials on American television, and this includes sharp controversy between them – a rare public situation in Britain. What can be said in general is that the transmissive elements of television are more widely used in American practice: an interpretation in terms of access.

In British television, where this kind of access and entry is much less common, there is on the other hand a much wider area of specially arranged discussion and argument. It is not only that there are many more controversial features and documentaries. It is that in prime time on majority channels there are many more discussion and argument programmes. In current (1973) American television most such programmes – and there are really not many – are in public service broadcasting, and are characteristically presented through the personality of an interviewer or interrogator (*Bill Moyers' Journal*; William Buckley's *Firing Line*, *The Reasoner Report*, *Sixty Minutes*). The British range, from *Panorama* and *Twenty-four Hours* or

Midweek to *Man Alive, This Week* and *World in Action*, is not only very much wider; it is also more freestanding – more consistently an arranged service rather than transmitted access. This can be seen more clearly if we separate out the kind of programme which is most directly a continuation of an earlier form of public argument, the arranged and formal debate – in the United States *The Advocates*; in Britain several short-running experiments. Here the formality of the presentation as debate, with a chairman or moderator and certain declared rules of procedure, makes the special nature of the discussion explicit. In most British television discussions and arguments there are indeed some ground-rules, expressed in abstraction in the concepts of 'fairness' and 'balance', but these are normally dissolved into the actual presentation, and given little or no emphasis. What emerges, or is meant to emerge, is a representation of the state of 'informed opinion', with its own internal differences and nuances. There is then the paradox that though in British television there is more sustained and on the whole more serious discussion of public affairs than in American television, its characteristic process is at once consensual and substitutional. Certain producers try, at times successfully, to break this mode, and to develop it towards confrontation or the presentation of irreconcilable differences. But the majority tone and mode remain consensual, and the figure of the interrogator or the chairman develops into the figure of the true 'moderator'.

There is then the question of the relation of these processes of public argument and discussion to the orthodox representative political process. The most visible relation is one of tension. In the United States the Administration openly resents the power of the networks to present arguments from an independent position. In Britain there are continual allegations of party bias, this way or that. In relation to national leaders, American television still largely depends on or is limited to the form of the press conference, where the leader takes questions from the floor, and a status relation is then contained within the communication format. In Britain, by contrast, there are many more highlighted interviews and direct interrogations, often of a critical kind, where leader and interviewer are given positions of apparent equality. Directly transmitted public addresses, by leaders, are of course also used, in both kinds of television, on especially important occasions.

Yet there is quite another dimension of relationship between television discussion and the orthodox political process. To an important extent these uses of television serve to mediate the political process to its real constituencies. It is in this sense an *apparently* public form, in which there is reactive and specu- lative discussion of a decision-making process which is in real terms displaced or even absent. The exceptions to this are the direct American transmissions of public hearings and some of the direct British interrogations of Ministers. In these cases the public remains, evidently, beyond the screen; we are watching a proceeding which we can see as separate from us; we can then independently, though in effect silently, respond. But what more often happens is that a public process, at the level of response and interrogation, is *represented* for us by the television inter- mediaries. Not only the decisions and events, but what are intended to be the shaping responses to them, come through in a prepared and mediated form. These are apparently responses by 'our' representatives, though we have not selected them (as selected politicians, for their own defensive purposes, are often quick to point out). In any large and complex society this mediation of representation is especially important, since in its speed and general availability it tends towards monopoly of the reactive process, and is no less a monopoly when it includes an internally selected balance and differentiation of opinion. This is especially important in that it reinforces tendencies within the orthodox process of political representation, where represen- tatives, between elections, acquire and claim a certain absolute character; if we do not like *them*, and through them their policies, we can change them *at the appointed times*. There is then, in these different ways, a displacement and attenuation of representation which can be felt, at times, as its absence. Op- positional elements who are outside the existing structures of representation have to find other ways to present their views:

by petition or lobbying, directed towards existing representatives; or with much more difficulty, by actions and demonstrations directed towards the already 'represented' people. Characteristically, and in direct relation to the mediating nature of current television, many such efforts are governed by the attempt to become real – that is to say, to become present – in television terms. This is obviously true of the march or the 'happening', to attract the cameras. But there is then an obvious contrast, of a structural kind, between the apparently reasoned responses of the arranged studio discussion and the apparently unreasoned, merely demonstrative, responses of the arranged and marginal visual event. This is in its turn often mediated as a contrast between serious informed responses and emotional simplifying responses.

A powerful centralising medium such as television can then, in much the same way as the representative but centralising processes of government, exhaust and even claim to exhaust the necessarily manifold and irregular processes of true public argument. Orthodox politics exhausts it at a formally representative level. Television exhausts it at a reactive level. In relatively closed societies, this exhaustion can be almost total. In relatively open societies, it remains a tendency, but a very powerful tendency, since its means of arrangement and access are funded and permanently available, while alternative means are dependent on continual creation and recreation and in any case ordinarily lack its reach. The best television arguments and discussions are in fact those which open themselves towards people not assumed in advance to be already represented; for example, BBC 2's *Open Door*. Some of the worst, for all their internal skills, are those which *simulate a representation by their own criteria*. When this is, however statically, an attempted representation of public opinion, it can often be justified, within current institutions and techniques. But the criterion is more often likely to be a representation of *informed* opinion, and here a distinct social structure produces a distinguishable television form.

'Informed' is sometimes interpreted as 'having publicly

attested skills'. It is more often interpreted as 'having access to real sources'. What then materialises is in effect an anteroom to a court: 'informed opinion' is the White House correspondent, the Lobby correspondent, the political editor, the financial journalist. These are literally mediators, since their skills and knowledge (and therefore the dimensions of their discussions) are determined by the fact of access. Around the centralised and only intermittently visible processes of decision there develops what is at worst a session of political gossip, at best a session of café politics. Political argument is not so much heard as overheard, and the relation of these mediators to the centres of decision is duplicated in the relation of the audience to the mediators. This most powerful medium of public presentation is then in large part limited to what is at every level an intended mediation. The shock of vitality, when other conceptions of argument and discussion occasionally break through, is the best evidence of the deadness of the familiar and now orthodox routines of displacement.

(iii) *Education*

The lecture, the lesson, the demonstration and the class have all been taken over from educational practice into television. In many cases the possibilities of the medium have been extensively realised. Large audiences can be reached by exceptional lecturers and teachers. Visual demonstration of rare or complex material has markedly improved presentation of aspects of the physical sciences, of medicine, of geography, and of elements of drama and history. A developed educational service, such as the BBC or IBA or American Public Television schools programmes, or the British Open University, is a remarkable demonstration of some of the true possibilities of television. There are some obvious problems: the technical difficulties of clarification and questioning, and the continuing difficulties of making the student's own work active. It is significant that these have been best met when television has not attempted to exhaust the teaching process, but has been offered as an aid, in planned relation to the work of classroom teachers, or in planned relation to other kinds of material (as in the printed units of the Open University). These are uses which depend on and relate to an already organised educational programme. Yet the reach of television has understandably prompted other kinds of educational work: some of it aimed at specific groups (language teaching for minority ethnic groups in the United States or for immigrants in Britain); some aimed at professional and vocational groups; and then an indeterminate area in which educational broadcasting is distinguished from entertainment broadcasting, though it is tied to no specific group or course. In this last and very important area the forms used have often specifically and deliberately broken away from received educational forms, and must be separately considered.

(iv) *Drama*

There was a significant development of radio drama in Britain, especially in the War and post-War years, and at its best this was something more than straight broadcast transmission of known theatrical forms. Through the inter-War period there had been, in the theatre, several short-lived experiments in more mobile and flexible dramatic structures, as alternatives to the drama of the enclosed room which had been, since the 1880s, the dominant theatrical form. The work of Sean O'Casey in *The Silver Tassie*, of T. S. Eliot in *Murder in the Cathedral*, and the important experiments of the Group and Unity Theatres had made some real progress in experimental dramatic structures, but with only intermittent and short-run establishment in conventional theatres. Sound broadcasting, for the first time, gave some regular base for this kind of experiment. Much radio drama was still of an orthodox theatrical kind, but by the early fifties there was a significant body of new work, best seen in the broadcast plays of Louis MacNeice and, above all, in Dylan Thomas's *Under Milk Wood*. The new concept of a play for voices surpassed, in many instances, the limiting assumptions of an enclosed stage-as-room theatre. A new mobility in time and space, and a new flexibility in movement between kinds of dramatic speech – and especially between the conventions of 'spoken' and 'unspoken' thought and feeling – were important real gains. What could be seen from an orthodox theatrical position as the limitations of the broadcasting medium became opportunities for different kinds of dramatic creation.

With the coming of television as a majority service the situation again changed. It was possible to transmit performances of an orthodox theatrical kind, and it could be argued that the television play was the ultimate realisation of the original naturalist convention: the drama of the small enclosed room, in which a few characters lived out their private experience of an unseen public world. Since a major structure of feeling, in the art of the period, was in any case of this kind, it is not surprising that many television plays reproduced this assumption of the nature of representative reality. This was a drama of the box in the same fundamental sense as the naturalist drama had been the drama of the framed stage. The technical possibilities that were commonly used corresponded to this structure of feeling: the enclosed internal atmosphere; the local interpersonal conflict; the close-up on private feeling. Indeed these emphases could be seen as internal properties of the medium itself, when in fact they were a selection of some of its properties according to the dominant structure of feeling. Powerful work was then done on these bearings, from Reginald Rose's *Twelve Angry Men* (USA, 1954), through a whole range of isolating and enclosing plays to a late case like Ingmar Bergman's *The Lie*.

Yet for more than half a century there had been an especially interesting and complex relation between dramatic structures and the new technological means of production. It is significant that the most advanced drama in Europe in the 1890s – that of Strindberg moving towards *The Road to Damascus* and the Chamber plays – was employing dramatic means that were beyond the reproduction of an observed and static external reality. Indeed it is one of the most striking instances of the complicated relations between new forms of experience and new kinds of technology that Strindberg was experimenting with moving dramatic images in the same decade in which, in quite another environment, the pioneers of motion pictures were discovering some of the technical means that would eventually make this kind of dramatic imagery possible and in the end even commonplace. Strindberg was trying, against many of the limitations of the theatre stage, to create – as in *Dreamplay* – a flow of images which would be capable of realising some of the intense particular worlds seen under stress, in conflict, in personal isolation, in dream or in nightmare. In the experimental films of the 1920s, and especially in Germany, there was a direct continuity from these experiments by Strindberg, with new techniques that made possible the central mobility, fragmentation or dissolution of things seen, things remembered, things imagined. But in the 1920s, also, there was another kind of dramatic mobility. The enclosed room of the naturalist drama – the world of the private family or group – was exposed, by new techniques, to the public pressures that were seen as determining it: not just as *messages* from the streets or the stock exchanges or the battlefields, but as the dramatic *inclusion* of just these elements, in an indivisible dramatic action. Meanwhile the significant development of large-scale public dramatic action, in the cinema from Griffith and Eisenstein, had transformed our whole sense of dramatic reality and possibility.

By the mid-1950s – that is to say, by the period in which television drama became a majority form – each of these tendencies had gone through major developments in the cinema itself. Yet in some ways television was now replacing the cinema as the major dramatic institution. Public attendances at the cinema were falling very sharply, while in Britain, for example, by the sixties, there could be television audiences of ten or twelve millions for a single play. The new possibilities of television drama brought a significant creative response. The work of Paddy Chayefsky, from *Marty* in 1953, and of Reginald Rose and others in the middle and late 1950s, was the most creative contribution in all American broadcasting. In substance and in method – the exploring 'eye of the camera', the feel for everyday ordinary life, the newly respected rhythms of the speech of work and the streets and of authentic privacy (what was later described ominously, though it was intended as compliment, as 'dialogue as if wire-tapped') – this new television drama stimulated similar work elsewhere, though in the United States, because of sponsorship difficulties, it was shamefully cut short. The BBC's *Wednesday Play* series, in the mid-sixties, is the most notable British example of a similar phase of creative innovation and exploration. Though the surviving theatres still commanded and received cultural prestige, much of the best new work of the younger dramatists was by the mid-sixties in Britain going straight into television. It was predominantly a radical dramatic movement, drawing on and developing two major kinds of possibility: the drama of internal dissolution (David Mercer's *In Two Minds*) and the drama of public action or public-and-private tension (Dennis Potter's *Nigel Barton* plays). John Hopkins' quartet, *Talking to a Stranger*, explored the possibility of alternating viewpoints, in a family which was seen, in a sequence of four plays, from the points of view of its four members. There was also a significant and controversial development of drama-documentary: 'social issues dramatised' as it was ordinarily put; the best known example is Jeremy Sandford's *Cathy Come Home*.

All this work was uneven, but the vitality of American television drama in the fifties and of British television drama in the sixties was by any standards remarkable. In Britain by the early seventies it had not wholly died away; there were still many important local examples. But, as earlier in the United States, though within a very different immediate institution, several of the most creative producers and dramatists were pushed out to the margins. For it had been also, significantly, a social movement. The existence of very large audiences, for disturbing and controversial plays of this kind, was in many ways embarrassing to the broadcasting authorities and to orthodox public opinion. The single play, even when presented in a general series, was said, in a new conventional wisdom, to be 'difficult to arrange'. Under this and other kinds of pressure, a momentum was lost, perhaps only temporarily.

Yet at certain levels the whole situation of drama had already been transformed. What had ordinarily been, in the theatres, a minority art, was now a major public form. The cinema had preceded television in this, but in its high costs and in its tendencies to monopoly had been checked by deep social and economic forces. The comparatively low-cost original television play, which could quite quickly be shown to a very large audience, represented a new dimension of cultural possibility.

Yet the phenomenon of television drama has also to be looked at in quite another way. In most parts of the world, since the spread of television, there has been a scale and intensity of dramatic performance which is without any precedent in the history of human culture. Many though not all societies have a long history of dramatic performance of some kind; but characteristically, in most societies, it has been occasional or seasonal. In the last few centuries regular performances have been available in large cities and resorts. But there has never been a time, until the last fifty years, when a majority of any population had regular and constant access to drama, and used this access. Even within the last half-century, at the peak of popularity of the cinema, figures for Britain indicate an average of less than one attendance a week per head of the adult population. It is difficult to get any precise comparative figures for television. But it seems probable that in societies like Britain and the United States more drama is watched in a week or weekend, by the majority of viewers, than would have been watched in a year or in some cases a lifetime in any previous historical period. It is not uncommon for the majority of viewers to see, regularly, as much as two or three hours of drama, of various kinds, every day. The implications of this have scarcely begun to be considered. It is clearly one of the unique characteristics of advanced industrial societies that drama as an experience is now an intrinsic part of everyday life, at a quantitative level which is so very much greater than any precedent as to seem a fundamental qualitative change. Whatever the social and cultural reasons may finally be, it is clear that watching dramatic simulation of a wide range of experiences is now an essential part of our modern cultural pattern. Or, to put it categorically, most people spend more time watching various kinds of drama than in preparing and eating food.

It is easy to see the effect of this new and extraordinary scale of dramatic forms. Beyond the characteristics of the single television play, which have already been discussed, there is the significant and indeed central fact of the television series or serial. These have precedents in the cinema and in radio, and an earlier precedent in the serialised fiction of the late eighteenth and nineteenth centuries. But their recent proliferation has been vast. The *serial* is the more familiar form: a dramatised action divided into episodes. Most of the cultural precedents are for this form. The *series* has fewer precedents, and these are mainly in later nineteenth-century and twentieth-century fiction, especially in certain categories: detective stories, westerns, children's stories. Here the continuity is not of an action but of one or more characters.

It is clear that both serials and series have advantages for programme planners: a time-slot, as it is significantly called, can be filled for a run of weeks, and in their elements of continuity the serial and the series encourage attachment to a given station or channel. Many television dramatists now write episodes for serials or series more often than they write single plays. They then usually find themselves writing within an established formation of situation and leading characters, in what can be described as a collective but is more often a corporate dramatic enterprise. Certain formulas on which the continuity depends are then the limiting conventions within which they must work.

It is interesting to notice the highly specialised character of most of these serials. Police and private detectives, ranchers and cowboys, doctors and nurses, make up the overwhelming majority of the people seen. All these were already popular fictional types, before television. Yet it is doubtful whether, before the epoch of television serials and series, anything like the current proportion of dramatic attention to crime and illness had ever existed.

Yet there have been interesting serials of other kinds: in effect successors to the widely ranging realist and naturalist works of an earlier fictional period. In Britain *Coronation Street* is a distanced and simplified evocation and prolongation of a disappearing culture: the Northern urban back-streets of the depression and its immediate aftermath. More serious engagements with the run of ordinary experience, like *A Family at War*, have again often depended on an essential retrospect, and serials like *The Newcomers*, set in a New Town, proved more difficult to establish. One of the more successful attempts to engage with the run of contemporary majority experience was Irish Television's *The Riordans*.

Since their origins in commercial radio in the thirties, many serials have been dismissed as 'soap opera'. Yet their persistence and popularity is significant, in a period in which, in so much traditionally serious drama and fiction, there has been a widespread withdrawal from general social experience. The serial as a form now gets its prestige from dramatisation of well-known works; in Britain significantly offered as 'Classic Serials', and many of them re-broadcast in the United States, no less significantly, as 'Masterpiece Theatre'. This attempted blending of fictional and dramatic forms is interesting in itself. But the cultural importance of the serial, as an essentially new form, ought not to be limited to this kind of traditional ratification. Few forms on television have the potential importance of the original serial. If the form has been overlaid, understandably, by the 'classic' emphasis, and more generally by the stock formulas of crime and illness, that is a particular cultural mediation, which it is necessary to understand and look for ways beyond.

(v) *Films*

Widespread television came at a time when cinema attendances were declining: this development was in general one of cause and effect. It was then obvious that one resource for television programming was the huge repertory of already made films, and – after some early competitive withholding – these increasingly made their way into the schedules. They fitted, exactly, the model of broadcasting as the transmission of work which was already available. Under the effects of competition established film companies and centres eventually began making new films for television distribution.

But the media of filmscreen and television are only superficially similar. In basic composition there are many similarities, but in transmission the results are radically different. The size of the screen is the most obvious factor. In certain situations this difference of size can radically alter the effect of the image, though in other situations the viewer adjusts proportions for himself. Certain spectacular effects of battle and storm, of monumentality, and of overpowering close-up are lost or diminished on the smaller screen. Even more significant, perhaps, is the different light quality of the television as compared with the film screen. There are minor differences here between Britain and the United States, since in Britain, in many people's experience, the television screen is clearer, more luminous and sharper in definition. But this is still a matter of degree within an overriding difference. Much of the light-and-shade composition of the cinema film is lost in the dimmer, more blurred and more flickering screen of the ordinary television set. The planes and perspectives of much cinematic composition are again characteristically flattened.

The distribution of films through the television networks is then something different in kind from their distribution through cinemas. A degree of loss – in the case of some films, a quite unacceptable degree – is inevitable in present conditions. Yet to most viewers the film repertory of television is a welcome resource. I have often been told in the United States, and have at times felt myself, that the old movies were the only good reason for watching television at all. It is not only that many films hold up very well in comparison with directly competitive original television work, under present production conditions. It is also that the availability of so wide a repertory – from the endless stock features to the important films and the masterpieces – is a quite new situation for most viewers. The only comparable access is in quite specialised repertory film theatres and archives in a very few cultural centres.

Yet this advantage, which ought to be seen as absolute, is limited by two factors: the technical limitations already mentioned, and the character of most of the commercial distribution contracts. Some of the technical disadvantages are unlikely to be overcome, though there has been important work in adjustments of the speed of frames, and in transfer through special lens systems from film to videotape. The size of domestic screens remains as a major problem, but this is in part a function of the individualised character of television viewing. Of course a film that we have seen on a cinema screen loses much of its visual quality when we see it on the average television screen. Yet, equally, most television productions gain enormously when they are seen on the larger viewing screens which are available within the broadcasting organisations. I have seen a television feature, which I helped to make, in three different situations; on an editing machine, on a set in the home, and on a large viewing screen. The differences were extraordinary, and I found it significant that the least satisfactory experience was that of viewing on the ordinary set. Some of what are now described broadly as the 'technical limitations of television as a medium' are fundamentally related to the patterns of technical use in the home-centred small-set distribution system.

The problem about film distribution contracts is similarly related to the commercial character of the industry. What gets sold is a package: of a particular studio, a particular category, a particular director, a particular actor. Some of these packages are compatible with a form of programming that would deserve the title 'repertory'. But others are clearly forms of dumping: in order to get one or two films, half a dozen others must be bought; or in order to fill a 'time-slot' otherwise unsaleable material is indifferently acquired. The effects of this particular system on the television transmission of films have given the whole arrangement a worse name than it deserves, especially in the United States, where typical distribution (except on public service channels) is in any case subject to the extraordinary process of constant interruption by commercials and trailers. This very specific social effect, combined with the technical difficulties, has been built into popular generalisations about 'movies on TV' which in any real analysis must be taken back to their specific and in some cases alterable factors. It is all the more necessary to do this since, if some of the problems could be solved, the film could remain and could develop as an important popular art. In a more common and fashionable perspective, in recoil from the specific difficulties of current cinema and television distribution, the past and future of the film would be relegated to minority cinemas and to the archives. Characteristically – and with television seen as the enemy – there is much contemporary pressure for just this solution. But that kind of hiving-off, whatever its local attractions, would be disastrous for the future of our most popular modern art.

(vi) *Variety*

In orthodox cultural analysis there is a simple equation between drama and theatre. But this was altered in our own century, when drama was created also in film, in radio and in television. And before our own century there had been a significant cultural division, between what were called 'legitimate' and (if not illegitimate) 'variety' theatres. This goes back, significantly, to the Restoration period in Britain; it bears many marks of a consciously class-divided culture. Spectacle and the various forms of pantomime, usually contrasted with 'drama' – though of course with many mixed examples – are among its earliest forms. In the eighteenth and nineteenth centuries the variety theatre was intensively developed, at several different social levels. One of the characteristic forms of the urban industrial development was the music-hall, which in a very specific environment provided a mix of singing, dancing, physical display and new kinds of comedy. This cultural mix which developed in the variety theatres and then the music-halls is in many ways the precedent for an important part of television.

There was an element of participation in the music-halls if not in the variety-theatres; in some cases people could meet, drink and move about, as in earlier popular theatres; in many of the music-halls there was lively and continuous response. But this element of participation was only part of the new formation. Equally important was the discovery of forms which presented and interpreted the contemporary interests and experiences of the new audiences. Most drama, in the legitimate theatres of the period, was still not contemporary in apparent content and style, and in any case ordinarily belonged to a different level of social life. The variety theatres and the music-halls included contemporary experiences and responses at least a generation before the naturalist revolution in drama. Some of the material was seen, from the beginning, as belonging to 'low' culture. But in fact there was more significant dramatic experience in early and mid-nineteenth-century melodrama than in the 'high' drama of the same period. In some variety sketches, burlesques, extravaganzas and the like there was at least much more vitality. And in the music-hall especially there emerged a generation of solo performers whose line has since been unbroken: the performers we call entertainers and comedians. Their songs, monologues, sketches and routines have precedents in a long tradition of comic acting, but their presentation as individuals was in effect new.

These forms had, from the beginning, a mixed quality. The solo performer could be the man articulating elements of a new social experience, through a specific characterisation. In this respect there is a real continuity between an early music-hall performer like Sam Hall and a radio and television comedian like Tony Hancock. But the music-hall always included (and the variety theatres were built on) articulations of a different kind: the tinsel-and-plush spectaculars, deliberately offered to a relatively drab or deprived audience: those glimpses of 'high life', an expensively furnished display, which among the solo performers are represented by the succession of 'Champagne Charlies'. In the physical displays of jugglers, acrobats, ventriloquists and conjurers, all the traditional skills of professional entertainers found a new home; from the music-halls to the television screen is in these cases a true succession. But the 'high-life' displays are different; they were designed on the assumption of an audience which was on the outside looking in, and increasingly what was shown was not an actual fashionable life but, more interestingly, a spectacular exaggeration of its external assets, and in the negotiable forms of tinsel and sequins rather than, say, diamonds. This kind of display went through Hollywood cinema in the 1930s and is still a significant part of television entertainment: obvious examples include Liberace, most shows built around singers, and in Britain the *Black and White Minstrels*.

Solo performers of other kinds show direct continuities between variety theatre or music-hall and contemporary television. A significant proportion of what might abstractly be classified as television drama is composed in effect of variety-theatre sketches. Elements of melodrama have similarly been retained. The satirical sketches and revues of little theatres and night-clubs have found much wider audiences on television, though it is interesting that their popularity has often led to authoritarian pressure against them. Performers trained to variety-theatre and music-hall tours found obvious difficulties in the transition to broadcasting, if only because their material was used up more quickly. But shows were built around them, and a new generation of variety writers came to stand behind them. Along with popular drama and serials, these shows came to form the greater part of majority television.

In most of these cases there has been an adaptation of older forms to the altered technology and the altered relations with audiences which television involved. But there are some other cases: for example, the evolution of both the solo turn and the variety sketch into 'situation comedy'. In some of its forms this is essentially unevolved, merely adapted. But in some very significant and popular cases, from *Steptoe and Son* to *Till Death us do Part* and *All in the Family*, an effectively new form has been created and needs to be separately considered.

(vii) *Sport*

Television is said to be the medium and probably the cause of 'spectator sport', but this is a simplification. There have always been some kinds of spectator sport, from gladiators to bear-baiting, and there is a real overlap between the circus – itself a relatively modern form drawing upon older skills of physical display and animal-training – and the variety theatre: an overlap which is repeated in television. But 'spectator sport', as a concept in relation to other kinds of game, is a more complex phenomenon. It is now often said that gladiators, bear-baiting, the skills of the circus, are not 'sport' but 'entertainment'. 'Sport' is a description of other kinds of organised physical exercise: the games of football, golf, tennis, and so on. In fact, the old basic skills of running, jumping and throwing, generalised as athletics, were in many earlier societies 'spectator sports' in the sense that they formed the centre of organised festivals. Yet the development of spectator sport in the modern sense belongs to an urban industrial phase of culture. In Britain league football and the more organised popular forms of horse-racing began in the third quarter of the nineteenth century, and their development and expansion are indices of the development of a new urban leisure system.

Thus the extraordinary development of the many kinds of professional spectator sports in the twentieth century antedates broadcasting. Radio and television came to satisfy and extend an already developed cultural habit. Yet, in the extension, there were further effects. Televised sport has an effect on attendances at minor sporting events, and in some cases is controlled for this reason. In the last ten years, especially in golf and tennis, fixtures have increasingly been arranged for television, and this has had important effects on their internal and professional organisation, among other things bringing players much higher fees. These are the aspects stressed in criticism of television as an agency of spectator sport and commercialism, and some of the effects, including those of sponsorship, are undoubtedly important. In a number of cases, the old governing bodies of sports are being challenged or displaced by the new international commercial and sponsoring interests, with mixed effects. The sport may be better organised but it may also come to be associated with such irrelevant or even contradictory interests as smoking: the tobacco companies, responding to government controls on cigarette advertising, have been significantly active in sports sponsorship. Yet we should also recognise that regular televising of a wide range of sports has created new kinds of interest, not only among spectators but among potential participants. There is a large sub-culture of sporting gossip which takes a great deal of television time but which was already basically present in newspapers. The national and international sporting networks form a social dimension of an increasingly significant kind in urban industrial culture. In all these tendencies, and in their essentially varied effects, television has been a powerful agency of certain trends which were already active in industrial society, rather than a distinctly formative element. At the same time, some of the best television coverage of sport, with its detailed close-ups and its variety of perspectives, has given us a new excitement and immediacy in watching physical action, and even a new visual experience of a distinct kind.

(viii) *Advertising*

It is often said that advertising is as old as urban society, and it undoubtedly increased in the expanding trade of early capitalist societies. Yet there was a qualitative change at a much later date: in Britain in the late nineteenth century, related primarily to corporate developments in production and distribution, and to the attempt, following major trade crises, to organise rather than simply supply or inform a market. In newspapers, and on hoardings and billboards, advertising was already a major feature before the beginning of broadcasting. In some societies, such as the United States, it became the feature around which radio and television were organised, as well as the main source by which they were financed. In Britain it was as late as the 1950s in television, and the early 1970s in radio, that advertising became a feature of broadcasting. What in the United States was seen as a central element, determining certain qualities of the media, can be seen by this contrast to be a feature not of broadcasting itself but of its uses in a specific society.

The sponsorship of programmes by advertisers has an effect beyond the separable announcement and recommendation of a brand name. It is, as a formula of communication, an intrinsic setting of priorities: a partisan indication of real social sources. In some American series the advertising agency takes part in the selection and development of ideas and scripts, and this works both as a positive influence in content, and as a negative influence against certain themes and ideas. Again, to see international news brought by courtesy of a toothpaste is not to see separable elements, but the shape of a dominant cultural form. The insertion of advertisements in unsponsored programmes is a different formula; it has had, as we shall see, extraordinary effects on television as a sequential experience, and has created quite new visual rhythms. Indeed it is possible to see television of this kind as a sequence in which the advertisements are integral rather than as a programme interrupted by advertisements. This question will be discussed in more detail later.

Many television advertisements, especially on local and regional channels, are of an old kind: specific announcements with various styles of recommendation or invitation. Networked advertising is different; it contains some information but it draws on these other uses of the medium:

(a) rapidly dramatised situations, of an apparently general kind, in which the governing response – to pain, to anxiety, to the need to enhance attractiveness or pleasure – is sharply specialised to a brand product. Heavily concentrated on cosmetics, packaged foods and (more heavily in the United States than in Britain) patent drugs and medicines, it interacts through its styles with the kinds of drama – one might also say, the kinds of human simulation – which are common in 'programme' material.

(b) entertainment techniques, current styles of singing and dancing, which are reshaped to product recommendations and associations.

(c) picture-sequences of sport, leisure and travel, within which the product is inserted.

(d) the use of television performers, as themselves or in their character parts, to recommend products, or to be shown using them.

Television

The real continuities which exist between print and poster advertising and television advertising certainly need to be stressed. There are common elements of prestige recommendation and of emotional displacement (of a need or an anxiety or a fear or a wish) to a brand of product. But in television commercials there are powerful new elements of visual and aural emphasis, which can be fully understood only if their connection and interaction with non-advertising television material is recognised and emphasised. The reduction of various life styles and characteristic situations to fast-acting televisual conventions is thus a feature not only of commercials but of the kind of television within which they are important. The attachment of these conventions to a range of products can be separately analysed, but the particular specialisations to products and brands are in the end less important than the common conventional mode within which the definitions of need, satisfaction and anxiety are quite generally made. And these are evidence of the character of a dominant culture, in which needs and satisfactions are mediated, over a very wide range, in terms of commodities, rather than of a separable and marginal commercial enterprise. Because of the sequential and integrating characteristics of television in almost all its existing uses and systems, this organic relationship between commercials and other kinds of material is much more evident than at any point in earlier systems of advertising, and television advertising is in this sense qualitatively different from press and poster and isolated display advertising in any period (though the new relationship has been imitated in some recent colour magazines).

(ix) *Pastimes*

A surprisingly large amount of television, though more in the United States than in Britain, consists of programmed versions of earlier forms of game and pastime. Several parlour games which had in effect disappeared have been restructured as television shows, and use has been made of every kind of quiz and guessing game. In many cases the change has consisted almost wholly of public presentation of what was formerly a private group or family activity. The new features are the presenter (who has some precedents in the older masters of ceremonies) and, most significantly, the greatly increased prizes. There is a direct cultural connection between the ethos and the conventions of many commercials and these usually simple games played for expensive prizes or quite large sums of money. The games and pastimes of real groups are projected and enlarged as conventions of insignificant competition but now significant acquisition.

But there have been other and deeper changes. Shows like *The Dating Game*, for example, are conventionalised speculative mimings of various kinds of personal relationships: between prospective partners, husbands and wives, parents and children. The ordinary processes of human understanding, judgment and choice are turned into projected games for the entertainment of others: in some cases light-heartedly, as in some other and earlier social forms; in a significant number of cases in quite alienated ways, as the relationship is made into the material of deliberate embarrassment or prospective acquisition. There was an extreme case of this kind in a short-lived San Francisco programme which was in effect (since it used telephone call-in techniques) a use of television for prostitution. Some cultural line had been crossed there, and the programme was taken off (though there are several much like it in radio). But in one way it had followed, logically, from the kinds of presentation of people, as isolated and negotiable features and quantities, which are characteristic of many commercial television forms. Indeed, if the dominant mode of human perception and interaction is very generally mediated by commodities, though it has continually then to struggle with more direct perceptions and relationships, there is a real basis for programmes which present human beings and their detachable characteristics as commodities, either for purchase or, more generally and more discreetly, for window-shopping.

B. MIXED AND NEW FORMS

We have seen that there have been some significant innovations in the use, by television, of earlier cultural forms. We have already noticed, for example, the visualisation of news and the development of new kinds of dramatic serial, new kinds of selling conventions, new kinds of presented games. It is clear that television has depended heavily on existing forms, and that its major innovation has been their extension, which can be qualitative as well as quantitative. But to the significant innovations within forms we must now add some possibly new forms, which television has pioneered. There is rarely, as we shall see, absolute innovation, but some at least of these new forms seem to me qualitatively different.

(i) *Drama-documentary*

A new kind of drama-documentary was briefly noticed in the more general discussion of television's use of existing dramatic forms. But it is so important that it needs some separate emphasis. It relies on what is taken as an intrinsic element of television: its capacity to enter a situation and show what is actually happening in it. Of course in all such cases there is mediation: directors, cameramen and reporters select and present what is happening. There is thus an intrinsic overlap between what is classified as factual report and what is classified as dramatic presentation. This overlap is often confusing, and a good deal of attention has been paid to its negative consequences: the selection and distortion of news, the promotion or blackening of individuals.

Yet the overlap ought to be looked at also in its positive consequences. It may be easier to do this if we remember that in a number of arts – and especially in the film and the novel – there has been, in our own generation, a rethinking and reworking of the conventional distinction between 'reality' and 'fiction'. Already, in British television, there have been interesting 'mixed' cases: *Cathy Come Home*, *Three Women*. In American television there is the fascinating case of the serial *An American*

Family (1973). This was a regular presentation – as if in serial dramatic episodes – of the life of an actual Californian family, in its various aspects and relationships. As it happened, the wife in the family filed for divorce while the series was being made; it was said for quite unconnected reasons. I know that many other Californian families became deeply involved with this unusual presentation or exposure of the lives of a family of their neighbours. In general the presentation was 'undramatic'; there was no obvious editing, and some 'scenes' were correspondingly slow or disjointed. Yet the husband complained that it was all edited with a purpose: that of dramatising any row or difficulty. In its sustained use of what appeared to be a neutral camera, looking in on how an American family was living, the programme was a significant and intrinsically dramatic experiment.

It is certainly important to watch what is being done in each case, and it is probably right to say that there should always be frankness about the convention being used. But some of the complaint about 'confusion between reality and fiction' is naive or disingenuous. This attempt to hold a hard line between absolutely separated categories seems to depend on a fiction about reality itself. It depends also on the convention that 'factual' television simply shows, neutrally, what is happening. The real engagement of every observer in the events he is observing is doubtless a matter of degree. But it is so crucial and general a fact that its possibilities for creative television drama, of a new kind, ought to be directly examined, rather than ruled out by an ultimately untenable classification.

One of the strengths of television is that it can enter areas of immediate and contemporary public and, in some senses, private action more fully and more powerfully than any other technology. The neutral or would-be-neutral reporter is then at times a necessary figure, but his is not the only mode of attention. The true participant is often as relevant, and at times more relevant. To move from observing an action to sharing or communicating its experience needs to be a conscious step, but it is one that ought often to be taken. An editing technique can be used in either interest, and just as there should be social controls when accurate reporting is in question, so there should be social opportunities when it comes to creative interpretations. Some of the best experimental television drama has moved into this area. A line is crossed when actors are added to editing, or sets to locations, but there have been interesting occasional uses of both within the same overall form: actors and people in their own lives; places and events and their deliberate re-creations. What was being attempted in some expressionist drama (by the use of inserted newsreels) and has been successfully achieved in several contemporary novels and films, can then be practised in television over a wide range and with important qualities of immediacy. It is not, obviously, the only kind of television drama, but it may prove to be one of the most significant innovations in our contemporary culture.

(ii) *Education by Seeing*

Some of the best educational television, and indeed some of the best general television, has altered some of our concepts of teaching and learning. There is, as we noted, a good deal of transmitted teaching and demonstration. But there are many examples of what can best be called educational practice: the language 'lesson' which is simply half an hour in a foreign town, listening to people speak while we watch them doing things and meeting each other, in a whole social context; the natural history or geography 'lesson' which is in effect a televisual visit to some place where we can see as if for ourselves; the presentation of some other way of life, or some work process, or some social condition. These kinds of practice, which television makes possible by its range and scope, are directly related to some of the most encouraging methods within formal education itself, trying to experience a process rather than being taught 'about' it. They do not replace other kinds of education, but they add to them, and in some cases change them qualitatively, in what is clearly an innovating way.

(iii) *Discussion*

The extension of range in television discussions has already been noted. For most people, it is a significant cultural fact. But there have also been some innovations in styles of discussion, and these should be noted, since they amount, in effect, to new forms. There has been an obvious loosening of manner. At its worst, which is most often noted, this culminates in the talk-show or chatshow, where it is not what is said but that it is someone saying it which is made important. The contrived conversations to sustain the notions of 'guests' and 'personalities' are among the worst things television ever does, and on this scale this is new. But there are times in other kinds of discussion when a new medium seems evident: sustained and defined conversation, with a closeness of interaction that is made publicly available. Some of the best of this kind of discussion was developed in radio but television at times has added a real dimension to it: physical presence, attention, gesture and response which, when they are not merely spectacular or the devices of publicity but belong to the sustained, defined and developing interaction, can be, in their unity with the words, an experience that is significantly shared in some new ways.

(iv) *Features*

Some of the best work in television belongs to a mode which combines and extends elements of the essay, the journal and the film documentary. In Britain, where in the thirties the film documentary tradition was especially strong, there was some direct transfer to television. But the range of uses has become much wider. There is the personal television essay or journal, such as *One Pair of Eyes*; the personalised social report, such as *The Philpott File*; the television argument, such as Clark's *Civilisation* or Berger's *Ways of Seeing*; the television exposition, such as *The Restless Earth*; the television history, such as *The Great War*; the television magazine, *Horizon* for science, *Chronicle* for archaeology, *Aquarius* and *Omnibus* for the arts; *The Countryman* and *Look, Stranger*; the many reports of exploration and natural history. Taken in sum, work of this kind – I have given only British examples, for the mode is well established there – amounts to well over half of the best television now being made. Moreover, it can hold its own with some of the best work being done in any cultural field. In traditional terms it falls somewhere between serious journalism, especially in general periodicals, and the popular book, and it is at least as good as either in contemporary practice. Indeed in some important respects, where the visual element is central, it is the best work of this kind now being done anywhere.

(v) *Sequences*

Certain forms have evolved within the conventions of current television programming. In American television, with its extraordinarily short units and as it were involuntary sequences, mainly determined by commercials, there have been such interesting innovations as *Laugh In*, *Sesame Street* and *The Electric Company*. The comic effects of fast-moving disconnection, using many of the local techniques of commercials and trailers, made *Laugh In* in its early years a fascinating example of an effective form created out of a deformation. In Britain, in a different way, *Monty Python's Flying Circus* developed new kinds of visual joke out of standard television conventions, by simply altering the tone and perspective. *Sesame Street* is perhaps a different case. It has been said that it uses the techniques of commercials for education. Yet this is a doubtful description. Many of the technical possibilities for mobility of every kind were first exploited, at a popular level, for commercials, and have no necessary connection with that kind of simplified selling. Some of the best mobility of *Sesame Street* and *The Electric Company* is a way not only of responding to a highly mobile society but of responding in some depth, since the central continuities, within the fast-moving sequences, relate not only to planned teaching but to a kind of eager openness, a sympathetic curiosity, which is perhaps a truer social use of some of the intrinsic properties of television than any of the more fixed and confirming social forms.

(vi) *Television*

It is ironic to have to say, finally, that one of the innovating forms of television is television itself. So many uses of the medium have been the transmission and elaboration of received forms, or have been dominated by the pressures of overt content, that it is often difficult to respond to some of its intrinsic visual experiences, for which no convention and no mode of description have been prepared or offered. Yet there are moments in many kinds of programme when we can find ourselves looking in what seem quite new ways. To get this kind of attention it is often necessary to turn off the sound, which is usually directing us to prepared transmissible content or other kinds of response. What can then happen, in some surprising ways, is an experience of visual mobility, of contrast of angle, of variation of focus, which is often very beautiful. I have known this while watching things as various, in their overt content, as horseracing, a street interview, an open-air episode in a play or a documentary. To most analysts of television, preoccupied by declared or directed content, this is, if seen at all, no more than a by-product of some other experience. Yet I see it as one of the primary processes of the technology itself, and one that may come to have increasing importance. And when, in the past, I have tried to describe and explain this, I have found it significant that the only people who ever agreed with me were painters.

4. Programming: distribution and flow

We have looked at some uses of received cultural forms in the new technology of television, and we have looked also at some of the new and mixed forms which have been created within the technology. We ought now to look at the selection and association of these different forms in different kinds of programming. The concept of 'programme' needs, as we shall see, analysis. But it is useful, as a first step, to look in some detail at the distribution of varying forms of television within different kinds of service. We cannot properly speak of the uses of television until we have made these internal comparisons and contrasts. But it will then be all the more necessary to go beyond the static concept of 'distribution' to the mobile concept of 'flow'.

A. COMPARATIVE DISTRIBUTION IN FIVE TELEVISION CHANNELS

The distribution of types of television programme, in five channels – three in Britain, two in the United States – was analysed for a week in March 1973.

The channels are:

> BBC 1, London.
> BBC 2, London.
> IBA, Anglia, Norwich.
> KQED (Public Television), San Francisco.
> Channel 7, (ABC), San Francisco.

The categories used are conventional, as follows:

(a) *News and Public Affairs:* This category can be subdivided into news bulletins, general news magazines, news magazines for particular ethnic groups, and public affairs discussions. There is some overlap between these, at certain points, in that there are often magazine items within news bulletins, news announcements within magazines, discussion within bulletins and magazines, and so on. The significance of the figures, while occasionally interesting for the minor categories, is mainly in relation to the category as a whole.

(b) *Features and Documentaries:* These are as defined in 3, B, (iv) (page 75 above). It is a category not always easy to separate from, for example, news magazines and public affairs discussions. The normal criterion used is that an item is classified as 'feature' or 'documentary' when a substantial part of it is offered as direct presentation of the substance of a problem or an experience or a situation, by contrast with the 'discussion' in which a situation or problem may be illustrated, usually relatively briefly, but in which the main emphasis falls on relatively formal argument about it.

(c) *Education:* This is defined as items of formal educational intention, as distinct from 'educational' elements in other kinds of programme. It is subdivided into course-programmes for schools, colleges and universities; instructional programmes, not normally related to external courses, mainly on crafts, hobbies, etc.; and adult education of a more general kind – specific teaching of general skills, which is however not related to formal courses and qualifications. There is again some overlap between these categories, and the course programmes, for example, are available to and often watched by the general public. The total figure for education is thus more significant than the subsidiary figures.

(d) *Arts and Music:* This is a difficult category to separate, since it depends on received definitions of 'the arts' – painting, sculpture, architecture, literature – and 'music' in the sense of the established classical concert repertory and opera. It is given as a separate category because it is usually planned in these terms and is then significant as a received interpretation and as a proportion.

(e) *Children's Programmes:* This is defined as programmes specifically made for and offered to children, at certain special times. Children of course watch many other kinds of programme, but this separable category is significant. It is subdivided into programmes composed mainly of cartoons and puppet-shows; other kinds of entertainment programme, usually 'live' stories and plays; and educational programmes. This last subdivision needs explanation. Such programmes – *Sesame Street, The Electric Company, Playschool* – often use cartoons or puppets, and are often entertaining. But they are separately listed because their formal intention is to help with learning, and much specific teaching of skills is included in them, though often in informal ways.

(f) *Drama:* This includes all kinds of dramatic work (other than the special categories found in education, children's programmes and commercials). It is subdivided into 'plays' offered singly, even if under some general title such as *Play for Today* or *Armchair Theatre*; 'series', in which each play is normally self-contained but in which certain regular characters recur – principal characterisation, for example, thus building up through several items; and 'serials', in which a connected dramatic presentation is offered in several linked episodes.

(g) *Movies:* This is defined as films originally made for distribution in cinemas and movie theatres. Plays, series or serials which may in whole or in part have been filmed have been included under Drama.

(h) *General Entertainment:* This is a miscellaneous category, but as such significant; in Britain it is often grouped under a Light Entertainment Department. It is subdivided into 'musical shows' – where singers or groups are principally presented, at times with rather different supporting items; 'variety shows' – where the main emphasis is on comedy, in a number of cases with supporting musical items; 'games and quiz-shows' – where in many different forms there is some kind of overt game-playing or competition (often of the 'parlour-game' kind, in its many modern variants, often with members of the public participating) and question-and-answer shows of the same competitive kind; 'talk-shows' – a category not always easy to separate from 'discussions' and 'magazines' but conventionally defined as a separate form and presented as entertainment, usually late at night: in matter and manner usually strongly linked to 'show-business'.

(i) *Sport:* Televised Sport and sports discussion.

(j) *Religion:* Religious services, discussions and features, presented at specific times.

(k) *Publicity (internal):* A channel's presentation of its own programmes, by trailers, advance announcements, etc.

(l) *Commercials:* Advertising programmes of all kinds other than internal publicity.

The analysis is presented in table form, in hours and decimal fractions of hours. All timings have been carefully made, but it must be noted that in the absence of any published statistics of detailed programming, and in the absence also of any really adequate facilities for exact timing over several simultaneous channels, the figures are necessarily subject to some marginal errors. This is especially the case in relation to commercials and internal publicity, which break the form of the published schedules. In these cases spot-checks were made and then an average figure applied.

The figures as a whole are significant not so much for exact allocations as for purposes of general discussion and comparison.

Table 1: Programme Distribution by Hours

Sample week 3–9 March 1973	BBC 1	BBC 2	Anglia	KQED	Ch. 7
A. *News and Public Affairs*					
News	5·7	3·5	5·0	5·2	11·6
News mag. (gen.)	7·1	—	5·1	5·1	5·3
News mag. (ethnic)	3·1	—	—	2·5	0·3
Public affairs dis.	8·3	4·3	3·0	8·5	1·8
	24·2	*7·8*	*13·1*	*21·3*	*19·0*
B. *Features and Documentaries*					
Features	5·6	6·2	4·5	4·5	0·6
Documentaries	1·0	5·9	2·0	1·0	—
	6·6	*12·1*	*6·5*	*5·5*	*0·6*
C. *Education*					
Schools, colleges, etc.	17·9	16·5	10·7	18·6	
Instructional	2·9	1·7	2·2	3·5	0·9
Adult education	1·9	—	—	2·5	2·0
	22·7	*18·2*	*12·9*	*24·6*	*2·9*
D. *Arts and Music*	*1·2*	*1·7*	—	*4·5*	—
E. *Children's Programmes*					
Cartoons, puppets	4·4	0·1	1·1	—	2·5
Other entertain'nt	1·4	0·7	4·6	—	2·0
Educational	5·7	3·3	2·6	25·0	0·8
	11·5	*4·1*	*8·3*	*25·0*	*5·3*
F. *Drama*					
Plays	4·4	3·1	3·5	—	—
Series	6·3	0·9	8·7	1·0	16·3
Serials	0·8	1·5	8·1	3·7	6·1
	11·5	*5·5*	*20·3*	*4·7*	*22·4*
G. *Movies*	*6·7*	*6·6*	*12·3*	*5·2*	*23·8*
H. *General Entertainment*					
Musical shows	2·7	3·0	2·0	—	1·1
Variety shows	1·2	0·5	3·7	—	0·4
Games, quiz shows	1·5	1·0	3·2	—	15·9
Talk shows	2·0	—	0·9	—	15·0
	7·4	*4·5*	*9·8*	—	*32·4*
I. *Sport*	*5·9*	*1·1*	*6·7*	*2·0*	*6·4*

(Table 1 continued)

	BBC 1	BBC 2	Anglia	KQED	Ch. 7
J. *Religion*	1·1	—	0·6	—	0·8
K. *Publicity* (internal)	1·1	0·7	1·7	1·4	1·4
L. *Commercials*	—	—	10·8	—	18·4
Total Hours	99·9	62·3	103·0	94·2	133·4

Comment on Table 1

Of the five stations listed, three are public-service channels (BBC 1, BBC 2, and KQED), two are commercial channels (Anglia, Channel 7). There are differences to be observed quite generally, between television programming in Britain and the United States, but the most striking fact is a certain similarity of distribution within the public-service channels on the one hand and the commercial channels on the other. Since total hours vary so considerably, it is useful to express the distribution, by categories, as proportions of the total material broadcast. This distribution is shown in Table 2.

Table 2: Comparative Percentages in Programme Category Distribution
(to nearest half-percentage point)

Sample week 3–9 March 1973	BBC 1	BBC 2	Anglia	KQED	Ch. 7
News and Public Affairs	24·5	12·0	13·0	22·5	14·0
Features and Documentaries	6·5	20·0	6·3	6·0	0·5
Education	23·0	29·5	12·5	26·0	2·0
Arts and Music	1·0	2·5	—	5·0	—
Children's Programmes	11·5	6·5	8·0	27·0	4·0
Drama – plays	4·5	4·5	3·1	—	—
Drama – series and serials	7·0	4·0	16·6	5·0	17·0
Movies	6·5	11·0	12·0	5·5	18·0
General Entertainment	7·5	7·5	9·5	—	24·5
Sport	6·0	1·5	6·2	2·0	4·5
Religion	1·0	—	0·6	—	0·5
Publicity	1·0	1·0	1·5	1·0	1·0
Commercials	—	—	10·7	—	14·0

Comment on Table 2

Certain striking particular variations can be seen from this table – in particular in News and Public Affairs, in Education, in Children's Programmes, in Drama series and serials, and in General Entertainment. Indeed it is possible to distinguish two broad types of programming, which might provisionally be called Public Service (Type A) and Commercial (Type B). A comparative distribution of these types is shown in Table 3.

Table 3: Comparative Percentages of Types of Programming
       (to nearest half-percentage point)

Type A: News and Public Affairs, Features and Documentaries, Education, Arts and Music, Children's Programmes, Plays.

Type B: Drama series and serials, movies, general entertainment.

Sample week 3–9 March 1973	BBC 1	BBC 2	Anglia	KQED	Ch. 7
Type A	71	75	42·9	86	20·5
Type B	21	22·5	38·1	10·5	59·5

Comment on Table 3

If comparisons are made only between the British channels or between the American channels, the distinction between Public Service Television (Type A) and Commercial Television (Type B) is especially clear. Yet when all five channels are compared, it is clear that the situation in American television is more sharply polarised. The American commercial channel (Channel 7) is a more complete representation of the predominantly commercial distribution than its British counterpart (Anglia) which shows some of the same tendencies but is midway between the British public-service type (BBC 1 and 2) and the American commercial type. Correspondingly, the American public-service channel (KQED) is more markedly of a public-service type, and in that sense less of a general broadcasting service, than its British public-service counterparts.

General Comment on Tables *1*, *2* and *3*

Tables of distribution by categories can show us some significant features of the uses of television in different kinds of broadcasting institutions. Moreover, some of these features are significant indicators of quality. But some are not, and we must try to make this clear, as a way of seeing beyond simple equations of quality and type.

Thus a category such as drama serials can vary from 'classic serials' and 'masterpiece theatre' to what is still, in very much the original terms, 'soap opera'. Movies, obviously, can vary enormously, from routine productions to significant works in the film repertory. It is true to say that distribution, in these respects, often follows the general tendency of the programming, but in the case of movies, especially, this is by no means universally so. A film on KQED is likely to be of the 'repertory' type, and serials on KQED and BBC 2 of the 'classic' type, while serials on Anglia and Channel 7 are quite often 'soap-opera'. But there is no such distinction between the selection of movies on, for example, BBC 1 and Anglia and Channel 7. The same general point holds for games and quizzes. In general those on BBC 1 and BBC 2 offer themselves as of a 'cultural' type, while those on Channel 7 are wholly commercial in conception and presentation and those on Anglia vary between the two kinds. There is some real variation of quality here: *University Challenge* and *Top of the Form* are in real respects different from *The Golden Shot* and *Double Your Money*. But the difference does not necessarily hold for games like *Call my Bluff*, where the surface material – the meanings of rare words – is 'cultural' but the essential presentation is a matter of straight show-business.

What can be discerned, indeed, is not only a general distinction between 'cultural' and 'commercial' programmes – of the kind roughly indicated by Type A and Type B programming – but also an equally significant cultural 'set' in each type of programming. Thus Type A is based not only on assumptions about education and the learning process – though these are evident – but also on characteristic definitions of public and general interest which often, on analysis, show themselves as essentially abstract and at times merely passive. In Type B there are evident assumptions of entertainment and distraction, but these involve definitions of interest which are sometimes more closely centred on individually presented persons and on a kind of participation (these elements are particularly evident in some of the serials and in some of the relationship games). It is then only on the assumption of a particular cultural 'set' – itself related to the character of education and daily life, and containing within it quite evident class characteristics – that one can assume that, for example, a documentary on international aviation is more *serious* than a serial or a game involving the presentation of a relationship between husbands and wives or parents and children. The mode of attention in each case has a specific character, and if the latter is trivialised or vitiated by a manner of presentation, so may the former be abstracted and in its own way trivialised by its more conventionally 'serious' abstract examination. That is why, though the distribution shown and the broad distinction between types are necessary elements of analysis, they are only one kind of analysis of real content, either generally or in terms of the particular television experience. It is then to another mode of analysis that we must now turn.

B. PROGRAMMING AS SEQUENCE OR FLOW

Analysis of a distribution of interest or categories in a broadcasting programme, while in its own terms significant, is necessarily abstract and static. In all developed broadcasting systems the characteristic organisation, and therefore the characteristic experience, is one of sequence or flow. This phenomenon, of planned flow, is then perhaps the defining characteristic of broadcasting, simultaneously as a technology and as a cultural form.

In all communications systems before broadcasting the essential items were discrete. A book or a pamphlet was taken and read as a specific item. A meeting occurred at a particular date and place. A play was performed in a particular theatre at a set hour. The difference in broadcasting is not only that these events, or events resembling them, are available inside the home, by the operation of a switch. It is that the real programme that is offered is a *sequence* or set of alternative sequences of these and other similar events, which are then available in a single dimension and in a single operation.

Yet we have become so used to this that in a way we do not see it. Most of our habitual vocabulary of response and description has been shaped by the experience of discrete events. We have developed ways of responding to a particular book or a particular play, drawing on our experience of other books and plays. When we go out to a meeting or a concert or a game we take other experience with us and we return to other experience, but the specific event is ordinarily an occasion, setting up its own internal conditions and responses. Our most general modes of comprehension and judgment are then closely linked to these kinds of specific and isolated, temporary, forms of attention.

Some earlier kinds of communication contained, it is true, internal variation and at times miscellaneity. Dramatic performances included musical interludes, or the main play was preceded by a curtain-raiser. In print there are such characteristic forms as the almanac and the chapbook, which include items relating to very different kinds of interest and involving quite different kinds of response. The magazine, invented as a specific form in the early eighteenth century, was designed as a miscellany, mainly for a new and expanding and culturally inexperienced middle-class audience. The modern newspaper, from the eighteenth century but very much more markedly from the nineteenth century, became a miscellany, not only of news items that were often essentially unrelated, but of features, anecdotes, drawings, photographs and advertisements. From the late nineteenth century this came to be reflected in formal layout, culminating in the characteristic jigsaw effect of the modern newspaper page. Meanwhile, sporting events, especially football matches, as they became increasingly important public occasions, included entertainment such as music or marching in their intervals.

This general trend, towards an increasing variability and miscellaneity of public communications, is evidently part of a whole social experience. It has profound connections with the growth and development of greater physical and social mobility, in conditions both of cultural expansion and of consumer rather than community cultural organisation. Yet until the coming of broadcasting the normal expectation was still of a discrete event or of a succession of discrete events. People took a book or a pamphlet or a newspaper, went out to a play or a concert or a meeting or a match, with a single predominant expectation and attitude. The social relationships set up in these various cultural events were specific and in some degree temporary.

Broadcasting, in its earliest stages, inherited this tradition and worked mainly within it. Broadcasters discovered the kinds of thing they could do or, as some of them would still normally say, transmit. The musical concert could be broadcast or arranged for broadcasting. The public address – the lecture or the sermon, the speech at a meeting – could be broadcast as a talk. The sports match could be described and shown. The play could be performed, in this new theatre of the air. Then as the service extended, these items, still considered as discrete units, were assembled into programmes. The word 'programme' is characteristic, with its traditional bases in theatre and music-hall. With increasing organisation, as the service extended, this 'programme' became a series of timed units. Each unit could be thought of discretely, and the work of programming was a serial assembly of these units. Problems of mix and proportion became predominant in broadcasting policy. Characteristically, as most clearly in the development of British sound broadcasting, there was a steady evolution from a general service, with its internal criteria of mix and proportion and what was called 'balance', to contrasting types of service, alternative programmes. 'Home', 'Light' and 'Third', in British radio, were the eventual names

for what were privately described and indeed generally understood as 'general', 'popular' and 'educated' broadcasting.
Problems of mix and proportion, formerly considered within a
single service, were then basically transferred to a range of
alternative programmes, corresponding to assumed social and
educational levels. This tendency was taken further in later
forms of reorganisation, as in the present specialised British
radio services One to Four. In an American radio programme
listing, which is before me as I write, there is a further specialisation: the predominantly musical programmes are briefly characterised, by wavelength, as 'rock', 'country', 'classical', 'nostalgic'
and so on. In one sense this can be traced as a development of
programming: extensions of the service have brought further
degrees of rationalisation and specialisation.

But the development can also be seen, and in my view needs
to be seen, in quite other ways. There has been a significant
shift from the concept of sequence as *programming* to the concept
of sequence as *flow*. Yet this is difficult to see because the older
concept of programming – the temporal sequence within which
mix and proportion and balance operate – is still active and still
to some extent real.

What is it then that has been decisively altered? A broadcasting
programme, on sound or television, is still formally a series of
timed units. What is published as information about the broadcasting services is still of this kind: we can look up the time of a
particular 'show' or 'programme'; we can turn on for that item;
we can select and respond to it discretely.

Yet for all the familiarity of this model, the normal experience
of broadcasting, when we really consider it, is different. And
indeed this is recognised in the ways we speak of 'watching
television', 'listening to the radio', picking on the general rather
than the specific experience. This has been true of all broadcasting, but some significant internal developments have greatly
reinforced it. These developments can be indicated in one simple
way. In earlier phases of the broadcasting service, both in
sound and television, there were *intervals* between programme
units: true intervals, usually marked by some conventional

sound or picture to show that the general service was still active. There was the sound of bells or the sight of waves breaking, and these marked the intervals between discrete programme units. There is still a residual example of this type in the turning globe which functions as an interval signal in BBC television.

But in most television services, as they are currently operated, the concept of the interval – though still, for certain purposes, retained as a concept – has been fundamentally revalued. This change came about in two ways, which are still unevenly represented in different services. The decisive innovation was in services financed by commercial advertising. The intervals between programme units were obvious places for the advertising to be included. In British commercial television there was a specific and formal undertaking that 'programmes' should not be interrupted by advertising; this could take place only in 'natural breaks': between the movements of a symphony, or between the acts in *Hamlet*, as the Government spokesman said in the House of Lords! In practice, of course, this was never complied with, nor was it ever intended that it should be. A 'natural break' became any moment of convenient insertion. News programmes, plays, even films that had been shown in cinemas as specific whole performances, began to be interrupted for commercials. On American television this development was different; the sponsored programmes incorporated the advertising from the outset, from the initial conception, as part of the whole package. But it is now obvious, in both British and American commercial television, that the notion of 'interruption', while it has still some residual force from an older model, has become inadequate. What is being offered is not, in older terms, a programme of discrete units with particular insertions, but a planned flow, in which the true series is not the published sequence of programme items but this sequence transformed by the inclusion of another kind of sequence, so that these sequences together compose the real flow, the real 'broadcasting'. Increasingly, in both commercial and public-service television, a further sequence was added: trailers of programmes to be shown at some later time or on some later day, or more itemised programme news. This was intensified in conditions of competition, when it became important to broadcasting planners to retain viewers – or as they put it, to 'capture' them – for a whole evening's sequence. And with the eventual unification of these two or three sequences, a new kind of communication phenomenon has to be recognised.

Of course many people who watch television still register some of these items as 'interruptions'. I remember first noticing the problem while watching films on British commercial television. For even in an institution as wholeheartedly commercial in production and distribution as the cinema, it had been possible, and indeed remains normal, to watch a film as a whole, in an undisturbed sequence. All films were originally made and distributed in this way, though the inclusion of supporting 'B' films and short features in a package, with appropriate intervals for advertising and for the planned selling of refreshments, began to develop the cinema towards the new kind of planned flow. Watching the same films on commercial television made the new situation quite evident. We are normally given some twenty or twenty-five minutes of the film, to get us interested in it; then four minutes of commercials, then about fifteen more minutes of the film; some commercials again; and so on to steadily decreasing lengths of the film, with commercials between them, or them between the commercials, since by this time it is assumed that we are interested and will watch the film to the end. Yet even this had not prepared me for the characteristic American sequence. One night in Miami, still dazed from a week on an Atlantic liner, I began watching a film and at first had some difficulty in adjusting to a much greater frequency of commercial 'breaks'. Yet this was a minor problem compared to what eventually happened. Two other films, which were due to be shown on the same channel on other nights, began to be inserted as trailers. A crime in San Francisco (the subject of the original film) began to operate in an extraordinary counterpoint not only with the deodorant and cereal commercials but with a romance in Paris and the eruption of a prehistoric monster who laid waste New York. Moreover, this was sequence in a new sense. Even in commercial British television there is a visual signal – the residual sign of an interval – before and after the commercial sequences, and 'programme' trailers only occur between 'programmes'. Here there was something quite different, since the transitions from film to commercial and from film A to films B and C were in effect unmarked. There is in any case enough similarity between certain kinds of films, and between several kinds of film and the 'situation' commercials which often consciously imitate them, to make a sequence of this kind a very difficult experience to interpret. I can still not be sure what I took from that whole flow. I believe I registered some incidents as happening in the wrong film, and some characters in the commercials as involved in the film episodes, in what came to seem – for all the occasional bizarre disparities – a single irresponsible flow of images and feelings.

Of course the films were not made to be 'interrupted' in this way. But this flow is planned: not only in itself, but at an early stage in all original television production for commercial systems. Indeed most commercial television 'programmes' are made, from the planning stage, with this real sequence in mind. In quite short plays there is a rationalised division into 'acts'. In features there is a similar rationalised division into 'parts'. But the effect goes deeper. There is a characteristic kind of opening sequence, meant to excite interest, which is in effect a kind of trailer for itself. In American television, after two or three minutes, this is succeeded by commercials. The technique has an early precedent in the dumbshows which preceded plays or scenes in early Elizabethan theatre. But there what followed the dumbshow was the play or the scene. Here what follows is apparently quite unconnected material. It is then not surprising that so many of these opening moments are violent or bizarre: the interest aroused must be strong enough to initiate the expectation of (interrupted but sustainable) sequence. Thus a quality of the external sequence becomes a mode of definition of an internal method.

At whatever stage of development this process has reached –

and it is still highly variable between different broadcasting systems – it can still be residually seen as 'interruption' of a 'programme'. Indeed it is often important to see it as this, both for one's own true sense of place and event, and as a matter of reasonable concern in broadcasting policy. Yet it may be even more important to see the true process as flow: the replacement of a programme series of timed sequential units by a flow series of differently related units in which the timing, though real, is undeclared, and in which the real internal organisation is something other than the declared organisation.

For the 'interruptions' are in one way only the most visible characteristic of a process which at some levels has come to define the television experience. Even when, as on the BBC, there are no interruptions of specific 'programme units', there is a quality of flow which our received vocabulary of discrete response and description cannot easily acknowledge. It is evident that what is now called 'an evening's viewing' is in some ways planned, by providers and then by viewers, *as a whole*; that it is in any event planned in discernible sequences which in this sense override particular programme units. Whenever there is competition between television channels, this becomes a matter of conscious concern: to get viewers in at the beginning of a flow. Thus in Britain there is intense competition between BBC and IBA in the early evening programmes, in the belief – which some statistics support – that viewers will stay with whatever channel they begin watching. There are of course many cases in which this does not happen: people can consciously select another channel or another programme, or switch off altogether. But the flow effect is sufficiently widespread to be a major element in programming policy. And this is the immediate reason for the increasing frequency of programming trailers: to sustain that evening's flow. In conditions of more intense competition, as between the American channels, there is even more frequent trailing, and the process is specifically referred to as 'moving along', to sustain what is thought of as a kind of brand-loyalty to the channel being watched. Some part of the flow offered is then directly traceable to conditions of controlled competition, just as some of its specific original elements are traceable to the financing of television by commercial advertising.

Yet this is clearly not the whole explanation. The flow offered can also, and perhaps more fundamentally, be related to the television experience itself. Two common observations bear on this. As has already been noted, most of us say, in describing the experience, that we have been 'watching television', rather than that we have watched 'the news' or 'a play' or 'the football' 'on television'. Certainly we sometimes say both, but the fact that we say the former at all is already significant. Then again it is a widely if often ruefully admitted experience that many of us find television very difficult to switch off; that again and again, even when we have switched on for a particular 'programme', we find ourselves watching the one after it and the one after that. The way in which the flow is now organised, without definite intervals, in any case encourages this. We can be 'into' something else before we have summoned the energy to get out of the chair, and many programmes are made with this situation in mind: the grabbing of attention in the early moments; the reiterated promise of exciting things to come, if we stay.

But the impulse to go on watching seems more widespread than this kind of organisation would alone explain. It is significant that there has been steady pressure, not only from the television providers but from many viewers, for an extension of viewing hours. In Britain, until recently, television was basically an evening experience, with some brief offerings in the middle of the day, and with morning and afternoon hours, except at weekends, used for schools and similar broadcasting. There is now a rapid development of morning and afternoon 'programmes' of a general kind. In the United States it is already possible to begin watching at six o'clock in the morning, see one's first movie at eight-thirty, and so on in a continuous flow, with the screen never blank, until the late movie begins at one o'clock the following morning. It is scarcely possible that many people watch a flow of that length, over more than twenty hours of the day. But the flow is always accessible, in several alternative sequences, at the flick of a switch. Thus, both internally, in its immediate organisation, and as a generally available experience, this characteristic of flow seems central.

Yet it is a characteristic for which hardly any of our received modes of observation and description prepare us. The reviewing of television programmes is of course of uneven quality, but in most even of the best reviews there is a conventional persistence from earlier models. Reviewers pick out this play or that feature, this discussion programme or that documentary. I reviewed television once a month over four years, and I know how much more settling, more straightforward, it is to do that. For most of the items there are some received procedures, and the method, the vocabulary, for a specific kind of description and response exists or can be adapted. Yet while that kind of reviewing can be useful, it is always at some distance from what seems to me the central television experience: the fact of flow. It is not only that many particular items – given our ordinary organisation of response, memory and persistence of attitude and mood – are affected by those preceding and those following them, unless we watch in an artificially timed way which seems to be quite rare (though it exists in the special viewings put on for regular Reviewers). It is also that though useful things may be said about all the separable items (though often with conscious exclusion of the commercials which 'interrupt' at least half of them) hardly anything is ever said about the characteristic experience of the flow sequence itself. It is indeed very difficult to say anything about this. It would be like trying to describe having read two plays, three newspapers, three or four magazines, on the same day that one has been to a variety show and a lecture and a football match. And yet in another way it is not like that at all, for though the items may be various the television experience has in some important ways unified them. To break this experience back into units, and to write about the units for which there are readily available procedures, is understandable but often misleading, even when we defend it by the gesture that we are discriminating and experienced viewers and don't just sit there hour after hour goggling at the box.

For the fact is that many of us do sit there, and much of the critical significance of television must be related to this fact. I know that whenever I tried, in reviewing, to describe the experience of flow, on a particular evening or more generally, what I could say was unfinished and tentative, yet I learned from correspondence that I was engaging with an experience which many viewers were aware of and were trying to understand. There can be 'classical' kinds of response, at many different levels, to some though not all of the discrete units. But we are only just beginning to recognise, let alone solve, the problems of description and response to the facts of flow.

C. ANALYSIS OF FLOW

We can look at some examples of flow in television, in three different orders of detail. First, there is the flow (which is at this stage still, from one point of view, only sequence) within a particular evening's programmes. For this we can use the general notation which has become conventional as 'programming' or 'listing'. Second, there is the more evident flow of the actual succession of items within and between the published sequence of units. Here notation is already more difficult, for we have to move beyond the abstract titles and categories of listing, and yet we are still not at the stage of the detailed sequence of words and images. Flow of this second kind, however, is centrally important in our experience of television, since it shows, over a sufficient range, the process of relative unification, into a flow, of otherwise diverse or at best loosely related items. Third, there is the really detailed flow within this general movement: the actual succession of words and images. Here notation of a kind is available, but it is still subject to the limitation that it notes as discrete (if then related) items not only the planned combination and fusion of words and images, but the process of movement and interaction through sequence and flow. Some of these limitations are, in print, absolute. But my examples are presented, with some commentary, as experiments towards some new methods of analysis.

(i) *Long-range analysis of sequence and flow*

(a) BBC 1, 14 JUNE 1973

  5.15 Children's programme: *Robinson Crusoe*
  5.40 Children's puppet-show: *Hector's House*
  5.45 National News
  6.00 News magazine: *Nationwide*
  6.45 American Western serial: *The Virginian*
  8.00 Film: *Chaplin Super-Clown*
  8.30 Documentary: *an Australian mining millionaire*
  9.00 National News
  9.25 Series: *Warship* (KGB official defects in Medi-
      terranean naval context)
 10.15 *Night Music*
 10.45 Public Affairs discussion: *Midweek*
 11.30 Late News
 11.35 Educational programme: *Mammals*

(b) BBC 2, 15 JUNE 1973

  7.05 Series: *Mistress of Hardwick* (Scenes from an
      Elizabethan life)
  7.30 News
  7.35 *Gardeners' World*
  8.00 *Money at Work:* The Gold Rush
  9.00 Film: *Little World of Don Camillo*
 10.40 Film Night: Review of James Bond films
 11.10 News

(c) BBC 2, 9 JUNE 1973

  7.35 News
  7.50 Feature: *Saboteurs of Telemark* (wartime)
  8.40 Serial: *Song of Songs* (Sudermann); early twenti-
      eth-century Vienna
  9.30 Feature: *The Ascent of Man* (history of science)
 10.20 Farce: *Ooh La La!*; late nineteenth-century
      France
 11.20 News
 11.25 Film: *The Razor's Edge*

Television

(d) ANGLIA, 15 JUNE 1973

5.50	News
6.00	News magazine
6.35	Serial: *Crossroads*
7.00	Quiz-show: *The Sky's the Limit*
7.30	American series: *Hawaii Five-O*
8.30	Series: *Romany Jones* (domestic comedy)
9.00	Series: *Between the Wars* (drama)
10.00	News
10.30	Magazine: *County Show*; ponies, vintage tractors
11.00	Series: Theatre of Stars: *The Enemy on the Beach* (wartime)
12.00	Sport: tennis
12.30 a.m.	Prayers for World Children's Day

(e) CHANNEL 7, 12 MARCH 1973

5.30	News Scene
6.00	National News
6.30	Movie: *Annie get your Gun*
8.00	Series: *The Rookies* (police)
9.00	Movie: *Doc Eliot*
11.00	News
11.30	Talkshow

(f) KQED, 5 MARCH 1973

5.30	Children's programme: *The Electric Company*
6.00	Children's programme: *Zoom*
6.30	Magazine: *Mission and 24th Street*
7.00	Newsroom
8.00	TV movie: *Winesburg Ohio*
9.30	Movie: Bergman's *The Silence*
11.20	Station publicity
11.30	Newsroom (repeat)

Commentary

These samples of 'an evening's viewing', on the five channels studied, correspond, in general, with the impressions gained from distribution analysis. The types of programming already described can be seen in their detailed sequences (two examples are given from BBC 2, because it is, in general, more variable than the others).

The specific content is in some cases worth special notice. There is a significant frequency of military material (much of it retrospective) and of costume-drama in BBC and Anglia programming. Anglia and (to a lesser extent) BBC 1 carry important amounts of American material. The BBC 2 mix is more cultural (and international) in its range, as is KQED, but BBC 2 is also quite closely attuned to specific English middle-class interests. Channel 7, as has been noted, has a limited range of largely pre-made programming.

The problems of sequence and flow are already apparent. Sequences (b), (c) and (f) seem designed for more conscious selection of particular items than (a) and (e) and especially (d). In (d) there is an evident sequence – in effect a flow – from 6.35 to 10.00 (a series of comparatively brief programmes of essentially displaced events and dramatisations), and the same might be said of 6.45 to 8.30 or 8.30 to 10.15 in (a). It is worth considering what effect, for example, the documentary at 8.30, in (a), and the series at 9.25, have on the News which comes between them: a certain definition of interests, of a characteristic kind, seems indicated. There would be a different effect in (d), where the News is preceded by retrospective drama and succeeded by the County Show.

The problems of definition of mood and attention occur in several of the sequences. It is noticeable that the sharpest contrasts occur in (b), (c) and (f), while there is a relative homogenisation – the most evident specific feature of flow – in (d) and (e) and to some extent in (a).

We can next look at some specific problems of sequence and definition, and from these of attention and mood, in what is in many ways the binding factor of television programming: the news bulletins and news magazines.

(ii) *Medium-range analysis of flow and 'sequence'*

(a) CHANNEL 7, SAN FRANCISCO, 12 MARCH 1973,
FROM 5.42 P.M.

... (*News Scene*; three announcers at desk; camera
alternates between general shot of all three and
medium shot of the one who is speaking; inset
for stills or drawings above, left)

I (Announcer 1)

A government committee has reported that many
claims in drug advertisements are false: one
brand of aspirin is not 'much better than another';
one brand does not 'work faster than another'.
(Inset: shelves of packets of drugs, still)
The committee recommends that 25% of the
time of drug advertisements should in future be
given to correcting these misleading claims.

II (Announcer 1)

A Senator has suggested that pharmacists should
display comparative prices of drugs.
Interview (filmed) with a pharmacist: he dis-
agrees; people should go to a store they trust.

III (Announcer 1)

(Inset drawing of food boxes and shopping bag.)
Consumers need all the help they can get, with
all prices rising. A housewife, angry at rising
costs, has sent the President four hundred
peanut-butter sandwiches, in protest against the
rising price of meat.

IV (Announcer 2)

(Inset, still, of Federal Building, San Francisco.)
There have been protests in the city against the
Presidential impounding of funds for projects
voted by Congress.
(Film of Mayor and local Congressmen)
The Mayor and the local Congressmen say im-
pounding is unconstitutional. The country

should be brought to a halt until this unconstitutional action is stopped.

v (Announcer 2)

(Inset: drawing of wreath)

The oldest Catholic Priest in the United States has died in San Francisco. He was 102. He attributed his longevity to brisk early morning walks.

vi (Announcer 2)

A mayor in Alameda County is working for a proposition to ban further apartment construction in his city. But his wife and six daughters are working on the other side.

Reporter (film of street in city; cars and houses): The proposition is being voted on tomorrow. The issue is legal and environmental. Further development, it is said, will reduce open spaces and lead to extra traffic pollution.

vii Woman (film: hand-spraying from can; table dusted). Liquid Gold furniture polish; brings new sparkle to your furniture; it's like meeting an old friend again.

viii Man (film clip): The 6.30 movie is *Annie Get Your Gun*. Betty Hutton as the sharpest-shooting gal the Wild West ever saw.

ix Weather forecast: (Medium, with charts). An area of high pressure, bringing in cold air.

x (Announcer 2)

In Utah, for the second time in a month, an entire barn has been stolen.

xi (Announcer 1)

Two strikes in the San Francisco area today; (Inset: still of Golden Gate Bridge)

one at an oil refinery; the other at a hospital.

xii (Announcer 2)

News soon about a man released from China and about the situation at Wounded Knee.

XIII (Film of cats eating)
Man: Little Friskies high protein cat dinners.

XIV (Film of women in home)
Man: Anacin relieves headaches.

XV (Model of house, with gold coins inside it)
Man and woman: loans available on house property in Bay Area.

XVI (Woman)
One-day sale at Macy's

XVII (Announcer 2)
A former CIA agent was released today from China.
(Film of man crossing border)

XVIII (Announcer 2)
Situation between Indians and Justice Department at Wounded Knee still tense.
(Still of Indian in headdress)

XIX (Announcer 2)
(Still of Château)
Pompidou is still President of France.
(Still of hand and ballot-box)

XX (Announcer 2)
Vice-President Agnew says there is no constitutional crisis.
(Film of Agnew speaking at meeting)

XXI (Announcer 3)
A murder victim in San Francisco has been identified.
(Film of police at scene of discovery of body)

XXII (Announcer 1)
Many reports of vicious dogs in the area.
(Reporter)
Farmers have reported attacks on animals.
(Film of dogs and film of sheep)

XXIII (Announcer 2)
The sports news will be next.

XXIV Man: if you didn't know this was freeze-dried coffee you would take it for fresh.

(Film: can undoing itself; cup being filled with coffee)

XXV Man: Let United Airlines show you this great land you live in.

Song: 'Come to your land.'

(Film: Golden Gate Bridge: girl singing

City street   : girl and man

Country fence   : two girls and man

Seashore   : group singing

Group travelling in plane

Black face close-up

Group travelling: song ends)

XXVI (Film: acted episode)

Crook: I used to be able to steal this kind of car. Now it has an alarm system.

He opens door: Alarm sounds: Sheriff appears. Crook shows key.

XXVII (Announcer 3)

Sports news: winning run by basketball team.

XXVIII Male voice (film clip): On the 6.30 movie, *Annie Get Your Gun*. Betty Hutton as the sharpest-shooting gal the West has ever seen.

XXIX (Network news: one man at desk; oblique medium shot)

A former CIA agent has been released from China.

(Film: group of men at border; ex-prisoner arrives at airfield; interview – he is glad to be back)

(Still: his invalid mother)

XXX Announcer:

In Vietnam, many permanently disabled men have been released from 'tiger-cages'.

(Film: disabled men in hospital; several emaciated and crippled; one crawling on floor)

XXXI   Newsroom
       (Title: ABC Evening News)

XXXII   Family camping in wood; children running under trees: the wife has brought margarine instead of butter; it is fresh and healthy.

XXXIII   Man at bank; in obvious pain. He is given a tablet in each hand; he walks away.

XXXIV   (Map of Wounded Knee)
       (Announcer): Situation still tense.
       (Film of car stopped and searched; close-up of Justice Department spokesman; close-up of Indian leader; Indian pointing to barricade)

XXXV   (Announcer)
       (Stills: Bermuda street; flags)
       Scotland Yard called in to investigate Bermuda murders.

XXXVI   (Announcer)
       A supporter of Peron has been elected President of Argentina.
       (Stills of Peron and Cremona)

XXXVII   Newsroom
       (Title: ABC Evening News)

XXXVIII   (Film): Truckload of television sets; one taken out; pictures shown on it, man talking; camera draws back to show more than twenty sets, each with same man talking.

XXXIX   (Cartoon): a fish jumps over the world; tinned tuna; woman eating from plate; fish jumps again.

XL   (Announcer)
       A government committee has reported that many claims in drug advertisements are false.
       (Still: shelves of packets of drugs)

Commentary

What seems to me interesting in this characteristic evening news sequence is that while a number of important matters are in-

:luded, the connections between them are as it were deliberately
ıot made. Consider, as examples:

   (i) the lack of direct relation between I, XIV, XXXIII and XL,
     which in any normal perspective are directly connected;

  (ii) the lack of conscious connection between VIII, XII, XVIII,
     XXVIII and XXXIV, though one kind of connection had
     been made by the Indian demonstrations at Wounded
     Knee;

 (iii) the lack of connection between the directly related items
     of political controversy IV and XX;

 (iv) the lack of conscious connection in the various items
     about prisoners, XII, XVII, XXIX, XXX;

  (v) the apparent unconsciousness of contrast in XXX and
     XXXII.

More generally, the effect of undiscriminating sequence can be
seen in IV–VI, IV–XI, as well as in the periods of 'interruption' by
advertisements, e.g. XI–XVII or XXII–XXVII.

Nevertheless, if the overall flow is examined, it can be seen
that a range of news and views – some reported, some propa-
gated, some dramatised – has in effect been fused into what can
properly be seen as a sequence. Items such as XXV or XXXVIII are
not incidental; they are among the controlling general images of
the flow as a whole – the perspective of the society, the practice
of the medium. The apparently disjointed 'sequence' of items
is in effect guided by a remarkably consistent set of cultural
relationships: a flow of consumable reports and products, in
which the elements of speed, variety and miscellaneity can be
seen as organising: the real bearers of value. Within this organisation, I, XIV, XXXIII and XL are not contradictory but are un-
paired alternatives; as are also VIII, XII, XVIII, XXVIII and XXXIV,
where the mediation, however, is more generally diffused. The
organised exclusion of certain kinds of connection and contrast,
as in XXX and XXXII, is part of the effect of the flow, with its
own more compelling internal signposting and directions of
attention.

(b) BBC I, 13 JUNE 1973, FROM 5.42 P.M.

     . . . (*Hector's House* – children's puppet-show)

  I   Dog puppet: 'I'm a gentleman.'

  II   (Local Announcer I): In *Look East* after the National News there will be a report on a new safety material for airfield runways. Also a report on a man who has broken the world speed record for beer drinking.

  III Clock.

  IV (National Announcer)
     (Still: Lord Lambton)
     Lord Lambton fined £300 on drug charges.
     (Reporter: against background of Lambton still)
     Report of case hearing.
     (Film: car arriving at court, men entering by special back entrance)

  V   (National Announcer)
     The ten-week-old work-to-rule at a Peterborough factory continues. (Aerial view of factory)
     (Reporter)
     Result of voting at workers' meeting.
     (Film of crowd raising hands)
     Interview with union official: 'We shall stay out.'
     (Film of factory and engines, as reporter continues)
     Interview with manager (office).
     (National Announcer)
     House of Commons reply to Peterborough M.P.

  VI (National Announcer)
     Pay strike at Cowley.

  VII (National Announcer)
     (Film of factory and pickets)
     Dispute at Chrysler factory.

  VIII (National Announcer)
     Britain's largest monthly trade payments deficit ever.

(Graph of deficit over recent months)
(Economics Correspondent)
(Background still of docks)
Figures very bad; reasons include floating pound, imports for industrial boom.

IX (National Announcer)
Prime Minister and TUC leaders have been discussing the economy.

X (National Announcer)
Agreement signed in Paris, between USA, North and South Vietnam, 'Vietcong'.
(Film: Kissinger signing; others signing)

XI (National Announcer)
Princess Anne's wedding date fixed.
(Stills: Princess and fiancé; Westminster Abbey; Archbishop of Canterbury)

XII (National Announcer)
Tribune Group of Labour M.Ps. say nationalisation must be included in election manifesto.

XIII (Still of Chief-Inspector of Constabulary)
Crimes of violence are increasing.

XIV (National Announcer)
Commons statement about terrorism in Northern Ireland.

XV (National Announcer)
Plans to disperse some government offices.
(Map and list of areas, with numbers)
(Still of Ministry and new town)

XVI (National Announcer)
School bus accident.
(Film of crashed bus, firemen)

XVII (National Announcer)
General Gawon of Nigeria has arrived in Britain.
(Film of reception)
(Film of his wife at children's hospital)

XVIII (National Announcer)
New safety material on runways.

(Film of aircraft running into foam bed).

XIX (National Announcer)

Rust makes car crashes worse.

(Film of test crashes of rusted and unrusted cars).

XX (Weatherman)

(Maps)

Warm and sunny.

XXI *Nationwide* titles: picture of baby in swing, lorry, baby lifted, car crash, man on phone.

XXII (Nationwide Announcer 1)

Later: Meet a man who talks to flowers.

XXIII (Nationwide Announcer 2 (woman))

Later: Two new reporters – children – report on toys.

(Film of children)

XXIV (New Announcer 1)

'All that and more as you move in to your own programmes, Nationwide.'

XXV Titles: *Look East*

XXVI (Local Announcer 2 (woman))

Decision at Peterborough dispute meeting.

(Film of meeting; voting)

Film of workers giving reasons for their vote.

Interview with union official.

Film of factory.

Interview with manager (office).

Interview with President of local Chamber of Trade.

XXVII (Local Announcer 1)

Work-to-rule at Wisbech; rail services disrupted.

XXVIII (Local Announcer 1)

Demonstration (film) against motorway plan.

XXIX (Local Announcer 1)

Claim of irregularities in local council election.

XXX (Local Announcer 1)

Bird's Eye factories expanding (film).

XXXI (Local Announcer 1)

A grave in Colchester desecrated. Black magic suggested.

XXXII (Local Announcer 1)
Two men rescued from dinghy.

XXXIII (Local Announcer 1)
Explosives found in pit in Cambridgeshire.

XXXIV (Local Announcer 1)
Norfolk deputation about by-pass.

XXXV (Local Announcer 1)
Huntingdonshire road accidents caused by uncut grass verges.

XXXVI (Local Announcer 1)
Peterborough Development Corporation selling houses.

XXXVII (Local Announcer 1)
Date of football match. (Still of captain)

XXXVIII Bishop of Ely arrives at a ceremony by boat.
Challenges another bishop to tug-of-war.
(Film of tug-of-war)

XXXIX (Local Announcer 2)
A young girl still missing.
(Still of policeman; still of girl)
(Film of road she walked on)
(Map of area)

XL Reporter: New runway safety material.
(Film: aircraft tests new runway safety material)
Interview with pilot.

XLI (Local Announcer 2)
Beer-drinking speed record.
(Interview: how fast? how many? why? – 'to break the record')

XLII Rupert the Bear at Yarmouth.
(Film of man dressed as bear on beach with children)

XLIII Closing titles: *Look East*.

XLIV Regional weather map.

XLV National weather map.

XLVI   (Nationwide Announcer 1)
Reporter: pyramid selling; new legislation.
(Still of calendar)

XLVII   (Nationwide Announcer 1)
Reporter: a community in Scotland where people talk to plants to make them grow; extraordinary success, no other explanation.
(Film of gardens)
Interview: director.
Interview: man who has seen an elf; the little people who live in plants.
Interview: gardener – he talks to plant.
Song: 'I dreamed a dream . . . of natural harmony.'
(Film of flowers)

XLVIII   (Nationwide Announcer 1)
'Back with a bump': decentralisation of government departments.
Regional reporters: Glasgow, Newcastle.
(Film of existing offices)
Interview with junior minister involved.
Regional reporters asked for comment (3-way discussion).

XLIX   (Nationwide Announcer 2)
Children (boy and girl) reporting on new toys; test them and give prices.

L   Closing titles:
Film of flowers repeated with song, '. . . natural harmony'.

Commentary

This is a characteristic British news and news-magazine sequence. It is more deliberately arranged than the American example in (a), and there is less apparently spontaneous reporting and commentary. The flow characteristics are strongly marked, e.g. II, XVIII, XL, or XXII, XLVII, L. The more intensive use of visual material assists a different kind of flow, with correspondingly less emphasis on the personalities of the readers (though in the magazine this emphasis is made). Within the flow, a characteristic set of priorities emerges, e.g. in IV to XIX. An item of scandal (IV) is placed first, followed by a group of items (V to VII) on industrial disputes. The most important item of general news (VIII) is then placed in a context indicated by this flow (though the direct commentary on it offers different reasons) and this underlying perspective is confirmed in IX. A related item, XII, occurs at a different and unconnected point. There is an interesting possible interaction, on a separate theme, between XIII and XIV. State ceremonies are dispersed between XI and XVII; accidents between XVI, XVIII and XIX (returned to in XXI, XXXV, XL).

There is a more general point about the overall emotional tone. Compare I, part of II, part of XXI, XXII, XXXVIII, XLI, XLII, XLVII, L with V, VI, VII, VIII, IX, XXVI–XXXVI, XLVI or again with IV, XIII or X, (XIII), XIV, XXXIX. The sequence XXXVIII–XLI is particularly interesting for its apparently extraordinary fluctuations, but the point is that this is contained – as are the other alternative normal sequences – by the fact of overall flow. A confirmation of this is given in the enclosure of the diversity and extreme unevenness of items within the playful emphasis of the initial XXI–XXII and the closing XLIX and L. This, essentially, is how a directed but apparently casual and miscellaneous flow operates, culturally, following a given structure of feeling.

(iii) *Close-range analysis of flow*
(a) (*Items* XI–XXI *from* (ii) (a))

(Inset: still of Golden Gate Bridge)

Announcer I   Well, there's still no progress to report on two major strikes in the San Francisco Bay Area today. The news from that Shell Oil strike at Martinez is – there is no news. All News Scene has heard unconfirmed rumours of negotiation not far away. Inside the plant supervisory employees are keeping the thing running smoothly, they say – in full operation as a matter of fact.

Strikers were also out today at San José Hospital,
(Inset: still of hospital building and pickets)
and late this evening News Scene had unconfirmed reports that Engineers' Local No. 39 have
also walked out.
(Medium: Announcer)
and in Martinez today too two doctors are back
on the job after they had initially been fired by
the County Human Resources Agency. The
County Board of Supervisors has agreed to re-
hire them and the terms of that negotiation
were hammered out in an informal session over
the weekend.

Announcer 2   Legal proceedings are now going on against the
(medium)   Indians at Wounded Knee, and a man in prison
in China for twenty years is a free man tonight.
We'll have film stories on those and other events
as News Scene continues.

(Film: music: cats walking in different directions)

Male Voice   Chinese or Persian, Calico or American Blue,
Angora or mixed, all cats want variety. And Little
Friskies has six delicious high-protein dinners
with a flavour that isn't artificial. It's made
from real beef liver, real chicken, real seafood.
- (Cats eating)
That's Little Friskies, the best tasting high-
protein cat dinners.
(Film: young woman at telephone, older woman
putting dishes in cupboard; rattle of crockery)

Young Woman   Will you please stop that racket?

Male Voice   When headache pain and the tension it can build
bring out the worst in you, take Anacin. Com-
pared to Anacin –
(Diagram: circle, with segment cut out)
– simple aspirin tablets would have this much
pain reliever. Anacin has –

(Rhythmic bleeps of sound; segment closes until circle is complete)

– all this extra strength to every tablet, rushing relief power to your headache. Anacin relieves headache and so its tension, fast.

(Film of women again; younger woman brings coffee to older woman; they sit down together) Anacin!

Young Woman I had the worst headache . . . (smiles)

(Model house)

Male Voice (2) If you own a house anywhere in the Bay Area, you're sitting

(Model lifts and gold coins pour out from front) on a goldmine

Young Woman (2) (smiles) and Pacific Plan will help you get the gold out. If you need from 1000 to 15,000 dollars, you can turn your equity into instant cash

(smiles invitingly)

by calling the girl at Pacific Plan. So, house-owners, dig into your white pages

(Still of telephone directory, focused on number) and get the gold out.

Young Woman (2) Call the girl at Pacific Plan today (smiles) or tomorrow.

Male Voice (2) Home Owners

(Model house: gold coins pouring out. Metallic tinkle)

get the gold out.

Woman (with flower on hat) This Thursday is White Flower Day at Macy's. It's one of the biggest one-day sales of the year, at all Macy's. (Waves) Don't miss it.

Announcer 2 (medium) In international news today, the very good news coming out of the Republic of China because a man who had been there for an awful long time

is finally out. Another prisoner of war free today, only this former prisoner
(Film of man at border post)
is ex-CIA agent J— D—.
He was a warrior of the cold war, he was captured in '52 in the People's Republic of China, on a spy mission. Today he arrived at Clark Air Force Base in Manila, a free man again on his way home to his sick mother.
The battle of Wounded Knee continues. The Sioux, who are holding a tiny piece of reservation, say they no longer recognise the United States Government
(Still of Indian, with headdress)
they say they've seceded. Meanwhile the Justice Department is considering legal action and it is very tense and touchy at this moment in Wounded Knee.
(Still of French Château)
And in picturesque France Georges Pompidou is still President of the Republic. Most of the Gaullist support came from the conservative French countryside. Still the communist and socialist representation doubled.
(Still of hand and ballot-box)
They cut the Gaullist majority to sixty seats. Big and sweeping social reforms now predicted for the Republic of France after this election.
(Announcer: medium)
Some very tough words today from Vice-President Agnew here in San Francisco. He told an audience it's up to Congress to hold back spending if inflation is to be halted, and then he also attacked those who say the President is getting too strong and usurping powers from the Congress. That's just not true, according to
(Film of meeting)

Vice-President Spiro Agnew.

Agnew Some members of Congress, abetted by certain eternally despairing commentators and columnists, are working diligently to persuade the country that a constitutional confrontation
(Applause begins; voice rises)
is at hand.
(Loud Applause)
And to support this thesis the Congress, according to a Washington newspaper, the other day brought in a collection of scholars for advice on its Constitutional crisis with Richard Nixon, and was taught that there really isn't any crisis at all.
(Announcer: medium)

Announcer 2 The Vice-President also wanted to say that he isn't aware that any Congress has ever felt sufficiently loved by a President to fully approve his exercise of power invested in him by the United States Constitution.
Steve.

Announcer 3 (medium)
Well, we have more details now of that grisly murder in San Francisco last night in which the body of a man was discovered by police
(Film of police in street)
in a metal container this morning. The victim's throat had been cut . . .

Commentary

It is only as we come really close to the substance of what is spoken and shown that we see the real character of television flow. A newscast is, of course, a particular case, but the kind of flow which it embodies is determined by a deliberate use of the medium rather than by the nature of the material being dealt with. As in the earlier analysis ((ii), (a)) the lack of demonstrated connection between items is evident. Yet connections of another kind are continually used:

... power invested in him by the United States Constitution.
Steve.

Well, we have more details now of that grisly murder ...

This order is predetermined, but is handled in such a way as to
suggest the continual arrival of reports. Most evident, perhaps,
is a sense of the announcers spinning items along, following a
rough schedule. They are clearly not reading from scripts (this
is a specific differentiation in American television news) but
they have certain cue formulas. At times these are of a distancing,
placing kind:

... the very good news coming out of the Republic of
China ...

... And in picturesque France ...

(In this latter case the phrase is determined, however curiously,
by the illustration.) Over much of the actual news reporting
there is a sense of hurried blur. The pace and style of the newscast take some priority over the items in it. This sense of hurried
transmission from all points is then in sharp contrast with the
cool deliberation of the commercials. At one level the average
length of a news item is in effect determined by the time-unit of
attention which the commercials have established. Nothing is at
all fully reported, though time had been found for the theft of a
barn in a distant state. Yet the flow of hurried items establishes
a sense of the world: of surprising and miscellaneous events
coming in, tumbling over each other, from all sides. The events
are caught as they fly, with a minimal and conventional inter-
pretative tag. The most ordered messages, with a planned use
of sight and sound, are the recorded commercials, which clearly
operate in the same communicative dimension. Voices are used
in both news and commercials to catch passing attention.
Devices of repetition to sustain emphasis within flow are
common to both:

The news from ... Martinez is – there is no news ...
Anacin ... Anacin ... Anacin ... Anacin ... Anacin ...
Get the gold out ... get the gold out ... get the gold out ...

The Battle of Wounded Knee . . .
. . . at this moment in Wounded Knee . . .

The sense (in general, false) of instantaneous, simultaneous
happening is similarly sustained:

> today . . . today . . . today . . . now . . . fast . . . today . . .
> or tomorrow . . . don't miss it . . . today . . . coming out . . .
> today . . . today . . . at this moment . . . today . . . now.

It is indeed the day's news, but taken emphatically on the wing.
If an interest can not be satisfied ('unconfirmed rumours', 'unconfirmed reports') it is nevertheless stimulated. In and through
all this, certain nodal references of meaning and value are given
emphasis:

> strikes . . . running smoothly . . . fired . . . rehire . . . free
> man . . . variety . . . extra strength . . . gold . . . free man . . .
> sick mother.

The selected preoccupations are the dominant *internal* currents
of what might seem, at first hearing (and there is usually only
one) a miscellaneous, even casual, *externally* determined flow.

The implicit meanings and values of the commercials require
a brief final comment. There is mutual transfer between their
formulas and those of separate programmes. The encapsulated
information of the news item is transferred to the mode of
recommending a cat food: 'high protein . . . isn't artificial';
compare 'tiny piece of reservation . . . very tense and touchy',
'still President . . . big and sweeping social reforms'. The mode
of the domestic serial interacts with that of the heachache-
tablet commercial, with the significant interpretation 'tension . . .
the worst in you'. The property-loan company relies on
memories of the historical film (this is in California): 'sitting on
a goldmine . . . get the gold out'. The breeds of cat, in the cat-
food commercial, are shown as in animal interest films. The
'instructional device' of the 'extra strength' in the headache
tablet is interactive with educational television and diagrams.

Television

The model house with gold coins pouring out of it is interactive with children's entertainment television. The girl inviting a telephone call (from a money-borrower to a money-lender) uses the look and accent of a generalised 'personal' (partly sexual) invitation.

In all these ways, and in their essential combination, this is the flow of meanings and values of a specific culture.

5. Effects of the technology and its uses

A. CAUSE AND EFFECT IN COMMUNICATIONS SYSTEMS

Since television became a popular social form there has been widespread discussion of its effects. The most significant feature of this discussion has been the isolation of the medium. Especially in advanced industrial societies the near-universality and general social visibility of television have attracted simple cause-and-effect identifications of its agency in social and cultural change. What is significant is not the reliability of any of these particular identifications; as will be seen, there are very few such effects which come near to satisfying the criteria of scientific proof or even of general probability. What is really significant is the direction of attention to certain selected issues – on the one hand 'sex' and 'violence', on the other hand 'political manipulation' and 'cultural degradation' – which are of so general a kind that it ought to be obvious that they cannot be specialised to an isolated medium but, in so far as television bears on them, have to be seen in a whole social and cultural process. Some part of the study of television's effects has then to be seen as an ideology: a way of interpreting general change through a displaced and abstracted cause.

Cultural science, when it emerged as a method in early classical sociology, was concerned with the necessary differentiation of its procedures from those of natural science. In its central concept of 'understanding', and in its sensitivity to the problems of judgment of value and of the participation and involvement of the investigator, it was radically different from the assumptions and methods of the 'sociology of mass communications' which is now orthodox and which at times even claims the authority of just this classical sociology. The change can be seen in one simple way, in the formula which was established by Lasswell as the methodological principle of studies of communication: the question 'who says what, how, to whom, with what effect?'. For what this question has excluded is *intention*, and therefore all real social and cultural process.

Suppose we rephrase the question as 'who says what, how, to whom, with what effect and for what purpose?'. This would at least direct our attention to the interests and agencies of communication, which the orthodox question excludes. But the exclusion is not accidental. It is part of a general social model which abstracts social and cultural processes to such concepts as 'socialisation', 'social function' or 'interaction'. Thus socialisation has been defined as 'learning the ways and becoming a functioning member of society', but while it is clear that in all societies this process occurs, it is for just this reason an indifferent concept when applied to any real and particular social and cultural process. What the process has in common, in many different societies, is given a theoretical priority over just the radical differences of 'ways' and 'functioning', and over the highly differential character of being a 'member' of the society, which in practice define the real process. The abstract notions of 'socialisation' and 'social function' have the effect of conferring normality and in this sense legitimacy on any society in which a learning and relating process may occur. And when this is so, intention, in any full sense, cannot be recognised, let alone studied. To say that television is now a factor in socialisation, or that its controllers and communicators are exercising a particular social function, is to say very little until the forms of the society which determine any particular socialisation and which allocate the functions of control and communication have been precisely specified.

The central concepts of cultural science – understanding, value-judgment, the involvement of the investigator – have thus been excluded or circumvented. This explains the consequent emphasis on 'effects', and the dissolution of causes into abstract notions of 'socialisation' or 'social function' or into the false particularisation of a self-directing technology. It explains also the orthodox description of such studies as the study of 'mass communications'. What is really involved in that descriptive word 'mass' is the whole contentious problem of the real social relations within which modern communications systems operate. Its merely descriptive and assumptive use is a way of avoiding the true sociology of communications, yet it is orthodox over a very wide range and in theories and studies which are otherwise sophisticated. A particular version of empiricism – not the general reliance on experience and evidence, but a particular reliance on evidence within the terms of these assumed functions (socialisation, social function, mass communications) – has largely taken over the practice of social and cultural inquiry, and within the terms of its distortion of cultural science claims the abstract authority of 'social science' and 'scientific method' as against all other modes of experience and analysis. Against this confident and institutionalised practice it cannot be said too often that the work of social and cultural science is only second-arily a matter of methodological procedures; it is primarily the establishment of a consciousness of process, which will include consciousness of intentions as well as of methods and of working concepts.

Effects, after all, can only be studied in relation to real inten-tions, and these will often have to be as sharply distinguished from declared intentions as from assumed and indifferent general social processes. This will require the study of real agency, rather than of its apparent forms. As it is, however, the study of effects has mainly been rationalised in advance. It studies effects in 'the socialisation process', that is to say in the practice or breach of social norms – 'violence', 'delinquency', 'permissive-ness', or in 'mass reactions' (a mass, to be sure, that is then classified into sectors) – the reactions of political or cultural or economic consumers, in voting, ticket-buying or spending. With this distinction however: that the latter studies have been mainly

Wants re-definition of terms & theories of practice

financed by interested agencies (broadcasting organisations, market research and advertising agencies, political parties), while the former have been mainly financed by social-interest groups and political and cultural authorities. Some studies have escaped the definitions of interest which their true agencies have imposed; in some universities, while there has been hiving and blurring, there has also been some independent initiative. But very little has escaped the overall definitions, including the definitions of procedure, which are the real consequences of the social system and the ideology within which the inquiries are framed. If we are to begin to approach any real study of effects, we shall have to return to a scientific consideration of causes.

B. SOME STUDIES OF EFFECTS

The case of 'violence on television' is a useful example. Here the experimental evidence is extraordinarily mixed (see the useful summary in Halloran, *The Effects of Television*, 1970; pp. 54–64). In majority it supports the view that 'the observation of mass media violence' may be, while not a determining, a contributory factor to subsequent aggressive behaviour. A minority view is quite different: that the effect of observing violence on television is cathartic. A further minority view stresses the possibility of both provocative and cathartic effects. Useful attempts have been made to distinguish, as is crucially necessary, between different forms of violence, different levels of its portrayal or representation, and different groups of viewers. There has also been a necessary distinction between immediate and long-term effects.

It is important that this work should continue and be developed. But 'violence' is a notable example of the effects of the abstract concept of 'socialisation'. It is assumed, for example, that violent behaviour is undesirable, in that it contradicts the norms of accepted social behaviour. But it must be immediately evident, if we look at real societies, that this is not the case. Each of the societies in which this work was done was at the time engaged in violent action – some of it of exceptional scale and

War etc. But socially acceptable violence.

intensity – which had been authorised by the norms of the society, in the sense of political decisions within normal procedures to undertake and continue it. At the same time, and for discoverable social reasons, certain other violent practices – notably 'violent protest' and armed robbery *within* the societies – had been identified and condemned. In what sense then are we to say that 'violence' is a breach of the socialisation process? The real norm, in these actual societies, would seem rather to be: *'unauthorised* violence is impermissible'. This would depend on a precise set of distinctions, within a given social system, between approved and impermissible forms of behaviour, and at the level of this true agency the identifications would never be in doubt and would indeed be rationalised as 'law'. (The law may punish you if you refuse to kill in a foreign war; the law may punish you if you kill or assault in the course of domestic robbery or internal political struggle.) This rationalisation corresponds to a particular social structure.

But then, while it may at that level be clear to the agency concerned, it may also, as it enters the communication process, be far from clear not only to the viewers but to the producers of its representations. Such confusion in viewers may indeed be separately studied: that is a discoverable and important effect. But it is at the level of agency and production that the real practices, and their implicit or possible confusions, require analysis. The ordinary assumption seems to run: 'this society discourages violent behaviour; violent behaviour is constantly represented and reported on television; we need to study its effects on people'. But surely anyone looking analytically at those first two statements would feel the need to examine their quite extraordinary relationship. Of course the apparent contradiction can be rationalised: the controllers of television are indifferent and greedy, governed only by the profit that can be made from programmes which show violence. (At a further level of rationalisation the medium itself can be reified: 'television finds violence exciting'.) But this does not explain the odd relationship between 'discouragement by the society' and constant representation by a major social communications system.

Television

Are we to assume perhaps that the television organisations are outside the normal social structure? But in all the countries in which the research is done the control and ownership of television systems is centrally characteristic of general social control and ownership and (in part) authority. When this is realised, it would be as reasonable to say: 'this society encourages violent behaviour; violent behaviour is constantly represented and reported on television, its major communications system'. But the truth is that neither assumption will do. What we are really faced with is a contradiction within the social system itself. And it is then to the sociology of that contradiction that we should direct our primary scientific attention.

A different kind of problem arises when we look at studies of the effects of television on political behaviour. These have been usefully reviewed by Jay G. Blumler (*The Effects of Television*, pp. 70–87). The centre of the problem is that a given society defines political behaviour in its own terms: in Britain and the United States, for example, as voting or as rating of political leaders. These have the additional advantage that they are relatively easy to count. Early studies seemed to show, moreover, that television had little discernible influence on either. Later studies, while not controverting this, found some measurable influence on information about party policies and, though it remains difficult to interpret, on the persuasibility of those with initially low party-political motivations or attachments.

But while it is useful to know these findings, and to look for similar further work, the most important question to ask is about the causes of these definitions of political effects. It is true that there is now beginning to be some study of 'system effects', as distinct from effects on countable individual voters. But this, too, has normally been undertaken within the terms of the political model from which the initial definitions were shaped. Thus it has been observed, correctly, that during elections but also at other times of general controversy, television as a system has become the most evident area in which political argument is conducted. Television interviewers and commentators have become, in a sense, political figures in their own right, and there has been evident tension between them and orthodox (usually elected) political leaders. Yet to the degree that elected leaders depend, or believe they depend, on television coverage, this tension does not prevent leaders submitting themselves to more open and public questioning of their policies than has ever been the case in any comparable communications system. This much, at least, is clear gain.

Yet it remains true that this kind of effect is within the terms of a given political system and its definitions of political behaviour. The competitive assessment of leaders and through them (but normally only through them) of policies is taken as a norm. But this at once raises a question. In Britain at least, during the period of television as a majority service, this mode of political behaviour has in fact been declining, in the important sense that the proportion of people voting at elections has been steadily going down. In the same period, other forms of political behaviour – notably demonstrations and political strikes – have quite markedly increased. It would require a very different model of cause and effect to inquire into this. It could be argued that increased exposure to competitive assessment in these terms has weakened adherence to occasional election as a political mode, or even that (given other kinds of political stimulation by television – the reporting of demonstrations, the dramatisation of certain issues) it has had some strengthening influence on alternative modes. Hardly anything is known about this, for the important reason that the assumption of effect was made, initially, in terms of the functioning of a given system.

Underlying orthodox investigation of the effects of television, whether on a matter like violence or on a quite different matter like voting, we can then see a particular cultural model, which tends to determine scope and method. What is usually asked about television is what influence it has by comparison with other influences. All these influences – television, the home, the school, the press, work – are assumed as discrete though then conceded to interact. Effects can then be measured, and techniques refined. But in an important sense there can be no inquiry about cause because the total social practice has been either disintegrated into these separable factors, or – an important condition for just this separation – has been assumed as normal: the *real* process of socialisation or democratic politics or what may be. Thus effect is ordinarily studied at a tertiary level, as between competing or alternative factors, and in the breach or observance of given social, cultural and political norms. Yet just these factors and norms are themselves effects; they are the established institutions, relationships and values of a given order of society. Primary causes, in the given order of society, are then ordinarily displaced by a doubtful sphere of effects taken as causes, with the study of effects then becoming, in real terms, the isolable effects of effects.

The particular importance of this, in the case of television, is that it reinforces tendencies to think of a given cultural system – the intentions and uses of a technology – in limited or misleading ways. That is to say, it studies the symptoms of the operation of an otherwise unexamined agency or – for this is the position which the former position in part prepares – it studies an agency as a system, in extreme cases performing the final feat of abstraction when it is supposed that what is being studied is simply 'a medium', 'a technology', with its own quite internal laws of cause and effect.

C. THE TECHNOLOGY AS A CAUSE

Sociological and psychological studies of the effects of television, which in their limited terms have usually been serious and careful, were significantly overtaken, during the 1960s, by a fully developed theory of the technology – the medium – as determining. There had been, as we have seen, much implicit ideology in the sociological and psychological inquiries, but the new theory was explicitly ideological: not only a ratification, indeed a celebration, of the medium as such, but an attempted cancellation of all other questions about it and its uses. The work of McLuhan was a particular culmination of an aesthetic theory which became, negatively, a social theory: a development and elaboration of formalism which can be seen in many fields,

from literary criticism and linguistics to psychology and anthro-
pology, but which acquired its most significant popular influence
in an isolating theory of 'the media'.

Here, characteristically – and as explicit ratification of particular uses – there is an apparent sophistication in just the critical
area of cause and effect which we have been discussing. It is an
apparently sophisticated technological determinism which has
the significant effect of indicating a social and cultural determinism: a determinism, that is to say, which ratifies the society and
culture we now have, and especially its most powerful internal
directions. For if the medium – whether print or television – is
the cause, all other causes, all that men ordinarily see as history,
are at once reduced to effects. Similarly, what are elsewhere seen
as effects, and as such subject to social, cultural, psychological
and moral questioning, are excluded as irrelevant by comparison
with the direct physiological and therefore 'psychic' effects of
the media as such. The initial formulation – 'the medium is the
message' – was a simple formalism. The subsequent formulation
– 'the medium is the massage' – is a direct and functioning
ideology.

There are of course specific characteristics of different media,
and these characteristics are related to specific historical and
cultural situations and intentions. Much of the initial appeal of
McLuhan's work was his apparent attention to the specificity of
media: the differences in quality between speech, print, radio,
television and so on. But in his work, as in the whole formalist
tradition, the media were never really seen as practices. All
specific practice was subsumed by an arbitrarily assigned psychic
function, and this had the effect of dissolving not only specific
but general intentions. If specific media are essentially psychic
adjustments, coming not from relations between ourselves but
between a generalised human organism and its general physical
environment, then of course intention, in any general or particular case, is irrelevant, and with intention goes content, whether
apparent or real. All media operations are in effect desocialised;
they are simply physical events in an abstracted sensorium, and
are distinguishable only by their variable sense-ratios. But it is

then interesting that from this wholly unhistorical and asocial base McLuhan projects certain images of society: 'retribalisation' by the 'electronic age'; the 'global village'. As descriptions of any observable social state or tendency, in the period in which electronic media have been dominant, these are so ludicrous as to raise a further question. The physical fact of instant transmission, as a technical possibility, has been uncritically raised to a social fact, without any pause to notice that virtually all such transmission is at once selected and controlled by existing social authorities. McLuhan, of course, would apparently do away with all such controls; the only controls he envisages are a kind of allocation and rationing of particular media for particular psychic effects, which he believes would dissolve or control any social problem that arises. But the technical abstractions, in their unnoticed projections into social models, have the effect of cancelling all attention to existing and developing (and already challenged) communications institutions. If the effect of the medium is the same, whoever controls or uses it, and whatever apparent content he may try to insert, then we can forget ordinary political and cultural argument and let the technology run itself. It is hardly surprising that this conclusion has been welcomed by the 'media-men' of the existing institutions. It gives the gloss of avant-garde theory to the crudest versions of their existing interests and practices, and assigns all their critics to pre-electronic irrelevance. Thus what began as pure formalism, and as speculation on human essence, ends as operative social theory and practice, in the heartland of the most dominative and aggressive communications institutions in the world.

The particular rhetoric of McLuhan's theory of communications is unlikely to last long. But it is significant mainly as an example of an ideological representation of technology as a cause, and in this sense it will have successors, as particular formulations lose their force. What has to be seen, by contrast, is the radically different position in which technology, including communication technology, and specifically television, is at once an intention and an effect of a particular social order.

D. TECHNOLOGY AS AN EFFECT

If we cancel history, in the sense of real times and real places, we can conceive an abstract human nature which has specific psychic needs and which variable forms of technology and intercourse come to satisfy. This purely idealist model of human history may have variable specific culminations – the end of alienation, the rediscovery of the tribe – but within it technology is a simple human effusion, the extension of a limb or a sense. The destiny and the process can be believed in only if we assume a human essence waiting to come to realisation, in these ways, with inbuilt if not yet realised metaphysical purposes. The model can be related to history only by endless retrospect, in which by selection such a process can be generalised or demonstrated. Characteristically, in such a model, there will be no more history: a culminating age has arrived.

Any cancellation of history, in the sense of real times and real places, is essentially a cancellation of the contemporary world, in which, within limits and under pressures, men act and react, struggle and concede, co-operate, conflict and compete. A technology, when it has been achieved, can be seen as a general human property, an extension of general human capacity. But all technologies have been developed and improved to help with known human practices or with foreseen and desired practices. This element of intention is fundamental, but it is not exclusive. Original intention corresponds with the known or desired practices of a particular social group, and the pace and scale of development will be radically affected by that group's specific intentions and its relative strength. Yet at many subsequent stages other social groups, sometimes with other intentions or at least with different scales of priority, will adopt and develop the technology, often with different purposes and effects. Further, there will be in many cases unforeseen uses and unforeseen effects which are again a real qualification of the original intention. Thus an explosive may be developed at the command or by the investment of a ruling class, or by the investment or for the profit of an industrial enterprise, yet come to be used also by a revolutionary group against that ruling class, or by criminals against the industrialist's property.

In other words, while we have to reject technological determinism, in all its forms, we must be careful not to substitute for it the notion of a determined technology. Technological determinism is an untenable notion because it substitutes for real social, political and economic intention, either the random autonomy of invention or an abstract human essence. But the notion of a determined technology has a similar one-sided, one-way version of human process. Determination is a real social process, but never (as in some theological and some Marxist versions) as a wholly controlling, wholly predicting set of causes. On the contrary, the reality of determination is the setting of limits and the exertion of pressures, within which variable social practices are profoundly affected but never necessarily controlled. We have to think of determination not as a single force, or a single abstraction of forces, but as a process in which real determining factors – the distribution of power or of capital, social and physical inheritance, relations of scale and size between groups – set limits and exert pressures, but neither wholly control nor wholly predict the outcome of complex activity within or at these limits, and under or against these pressures.

The case of television is an excellent example. We have seen that the complex process of its invention had specific military, administrative and commercial intentions, and each of these interacted with what were, for real if limited periods and in real if limited ways, scientific intentions. At the stage of transition from invention to technology, the process of its development came to be dominated by commercial intentions, though still with some real political and military interests. But then a primarily commercial intention acquired social and political intentions of a general kind, in notions of social training and social control which in part harmonised and in part conflicted with the driving commercial intention (the latter gaining ascendancy in the United States, though never an unqualified ascendancy; the former gaining but then losing ascendancy in

Britain, though again the loss is not unqualified). Yet as intention became effect another dimension opened. It was not only ruling or commercial groups who recognised the problems of communication in conditions of complex or of privatised mobility. It was also the many people who were experiencing this process as subjects. To controllers and programmers they might seem merely objects: a viewing public or a market. But from their own side of the screen there was a different perspective: if they were exposed by need in new ways, they were also exposed to certain uncontrollable opportunities. This complicated interaction is still very much in the process of working itself out.

Literacy had shown similar complications. It is interesting that at the beginning of the industrial revolution in Britain, when education had to be reorganised, the ruling class decided to teach working people to read but not to write. If they could read they could understand new kinds of instructions and, moreover, they could read the Bible for their moral improvement. They did not need writing, however, since they would have no orders or instructions or lessons to communicate. At most they might struggle to produce simple signatures, which would be occasionally required for official purposes. The full range of writing came later, with further development of the society and the economy. But it is what happened to reading that is really significant. For there was no way to teach a man to read the Bible which did not also enable him to read the radical press. A controlled intention became an uncontrolled effect. Yet the acquisition of literacy, then as now, almost always involved submission to a lengthy period of social training – education – in which quite other things than literacy or similar skills were taught; in which, in fact, values and norms were taught which became, very often, inextricable from the literacy.

The unique factor of broadcasting – first in sound, then even more clearly in television – has been that its communication is accessible to normal social development; it requires no specific training which brings people within the orbit of public authority. If we can watch and listen to people in our immediate circle, we can watch and listen to television. Much of the great popular appeal of radio and television has been due to this sense of apparently unmediated access. The real mediations will have to be noted, but again and again they are easy to miss. What is offered is a set with a tuner and a switch: we can turn it on or off, or vary what we are receiving. Throughout its history there has been this popular sense that broadcasting is a welcome alternative to the normal and recognisable social order of communications.

Many people who are aware of the manipulative powers of radio and television, or of its apparently inexhaustible appeal to children, react in ways which implicitly suppress all the other history of communication. Thus it is often indignantly said that television is a 'third parent', as if children had not in all developed societies had third parents in the shape of priests, teachers and workmasters, to say nothing of the actual parents and relations who, in many periods and cultures, intervened to control or to instruct. Against those real alternatives this switchable communication has profound attractions. Or it is said that people are exposed to propaganda by television, as if there had never been masters, employers, judges, priests.

It is interesting that many of the contradictions of capitalist democracy have indeed come out in the argument about television control. The British version of 'public responsibility' was an emphasis, in new terms, of the priest and the teacher, with behind them a whole dominant and normative set of meanings and values. The American version of 'public freedom' was open broadcasting subject only to the purchase of facilities, which then settled freedom in direct relation to existing economic inequalities. In each case the control theoretically lost by the switchable receiver was regained by the assertion of paternalist or capitalist ownership of transmission. This explains the realities of contemporary mediation, but it explains also the apparently irrepressible search, by listeners and viewers, for other sources. Many British working-class people welcomed American culture, or the Americanised character of British commercial television, as an alternative to a British 'public' version which, from a subordinate position, they already knew too well. In many parts of the world this apparently free-floating and accessible culture was a welcome alternative to dominant local cultural patterns and restrictions. Young people all over Europe welcomed the pirate broadcasters, as an alternative to authorities they suspected or distrusted or were simply tired of. The irony was that what came free and easy and accessible was a planned operation by a distant and invisible authority – the American corporations. But in local and immediate terms, as in the other cases mentioned, this did not at first greatly matter; a choice was being exercised, here and now.

Television has now been a majority service for a whole generation. It has had certain intended effects corresponding to certain explicit intentions, essentially declared by the variable character of television institutions. But it has also had unforeseen effects, among them the desire to use the technology for oneself. In the young radical underground, and even more in the young cultural underground, there is a familiarity with media, and an eager sense of experiment and practice, which is as much an effect as the more widely publicised and predicted passivity. Indeed, by prolonged use of a technology which had seemed to be contained and limited to commercial or paternal or authoritarian ends, many people – we do not yet know whether they are enough people – conceived quite different intentions and uses. This is the critical answer to the notion of a determined technology as well as the more ordinary notion of a technological determinism. For these new uses are at least as appropriate to the technology as the uses and intentions which have hitherto defined it. It is from this generation, raised on television, that we are continually getting examples and proposals of electronic creation and communication which are so different from orthodox television as to seem a quite new technology and cultural form. The town-meeting by television is a radically alternative definition of the relations between 'broadcasters' and 'viewers'. The multi-screen play is a radically alternative definition of the framed projection or the framed flow. Just as television was coming to seem a determined cultural form or a determined technology, there are these radically alternative definitions and practices, trying to find their way through.

How the technology develops from now on is then not only a matter of some autonomous process directed by remote engineers. It is a matter of social and cultural definition, according to the ends sought. From a range of existing developments and possibilities, variable priorities and variable institutions are now clearly on the agenda. Yet this does not mean that the issue is undetermined; the limits and pressures are real and powerful. Most technical development is in the hands of corporations which express the contemporary interlock of military, political and commercial intentions. Most policy development is in the hands of established broadcasting corporations and the political bureaucracies of a few powerful states. All that has been established so far is that neither the theory nor the practice of television as we know it is a necessary or a predicting cause. Current orthodox theory and practice are, on the contrary, effects. Thus whether the theory and the practice can be changed will depend not on the fixed properties of the medium nor on the necessary character of its institutions, but on a continually renewable social action and struggle. It is therefore to the immediately emergent problems of the technology and the institutions that we must now turn.

6. Alternative technology, alternative uses?

There can be little doubt that in the early 1970s we are already in a new generation of communications technology, and that much of this is centred on new forms of television. At the same time we are in a very contentious and confused situation about the institutions and social processes of all communications. There is still an unfinished struggle and argument over the institutions and control of sound and vision broadcasting: the conflict that has been clear for two generations between 'public service' and 'commercial' institutions and policies. It would be a major error to suppose that this conflict is over; indeed the signs are that it is now entering one of its most acute and difficult phases. But at the same time the actual and prospective development of new kinds of technology is altering some of the terms of this long-standing conflict, and may, if we are not careful, merely confuse it. On the other hand, some of the new technical developments seem to open the way to institutions of a radically different kind from either 'public service' or 'commercial' broadcasting; indeed of a different kind, in some cases, from 'broadcasting' itself.

We have then to try to clarify, first, the new technology and, second, the effects this may have on institutions, policies and uses of television. But we have to do this while remembering that the technology will not determine the effects. On the contrary, the new technology is itself a product of a particular social system, and will be developed as an apparently autonomous process of innovation only to the extent that we fail to identify and challenge its real agencies. But it is not only a question of identification and defence. There are contradictory factors, in the whole social development, which may make it possible to use some or all of the new technology for purposes quite different from those of the existing social order: certainly locally and perhaps more generally. The choices and uses actually made will in any case be part of a more general process of social development, social growth and social struggle.

A. THE DEVELOPING TECHNOLOGY

(*i*) There will be continuing development within existing television systems. As in capitalist industry generally, there is continual internal pressure to devise new forms of existing machines – the 'consumer durables' as they are, with unintentional irony, described. By definition these must be attractive or made to seem attractive to existing owners, so that a new wave of demand can be generated. The colour receiver was the last such innovation, and it has still some way to run. The portable television set is contemporary with it, and will be extensively developed. Micro-receivers are already coming into view. But the major development of the late seventies may well be the large-screen receiver: first the screen of four by six feet which is already in development; then the flat-wall receiver. This technology has a direct continuity with its immediate predecessors in sound and vision receivers, and even on its own it stands a good chance of remedying some of the faults of domestic television reception, with the particular advantage that it would directly serve existing mainstream television broadcasting, in an obvious alliance (already in some cases quite formal) of existing social and economic interests.

(*ii*) Cable distribution of television is, however, likely to attract even more attention. It began as a way of remedying imperfect general broadcast transmission: to bring signals to otherwise inaccessible or difficult areas, and to improve existing signals. Cable distribution is already widespread and is developing rapidly in North America. In Britain it is currently estimated that it will reach thirty per cent of the population by 1980; in North America it will be almost universally available well before that. On its own, cable distribution is simply an ancillary of broadcasting: picking up normal television on headend facilities; filtering, amplifying and retransmitting it. But two new developments are already in progress. First, a cable distribution system can become an independent broadcasting service: there are already many examples in North America, and some experimental examples in Britain. Secondly, a cable distribution system can be linked, via computers, with a range of services. These include, as probable developments now and on through the seventies and eighties:

(a) wired news, weather and traffic information services;
(b) shopping services, with the telephone system keyed in, so that goods can be seen and ordered;
(c) educational programmes of all kinds;
(d) 'demand' information services from libraries and memory-banks;
(e) 'demand' television programmes, films, etc. ordered from a library catalogue;
(f) 'telefax' or 'homofax' replication of newspapers, magazines and other printed material;
(g) medical consultancy services;
(h) public meetings, discussions, conferences and voting.

None of these uses and projected uses presents any major technical problem in itself, but there is dispute about the carrying capacity of various cable systems, and this question could become critical as the diversity of services, and especially of 'demand' services, extends. Most systems now in operation have a 12-channel capability, while some have 20-channel. A 40-channel system is in development. Many of the important decisions about channel-capacity equipment will be made in direct relation to the uses foreseen, and these will in turn be directly related to the types of institution controlling and directing them. There is also an important controversy about relative costs, as between broadcasting and cable, for different types of community, and this bears very closely on institutional solutions. Meanwhile an alternative method of short-range distribution, by quasi-laser systems, is at an early stage.

(*iii*) A related complex of visual information systems is certain to develop. These include the visual telephone – already in operation for conference systems – and a range of domestic devices from telereading of meters and telecast security alarms to developed systems of closed-circuit television, inside and between individual houses. These are relevant in so far as some of them may affect the design of receivers.

(*iv*) During the 1960s an extensive system of space satellite communications and ground-stations, including television, was developed. Much of the existing capacity is used for telephonic purposes, as 'common carrier', but there is a striking development of satellite television, both for relaying particular programmes and events, and as the means of a special service (already under way in India and in Latin America). Normal future development may be through ground-stations, which in receiving and then distributing signals will be in a position to select for transmission within the areas they cover. But it is estimated that by the mid-seventies direct transmission into augmented home receivers will be technically possible, though costly. Prototype models already exist, including in Britain. Transmission into unaugmented domestic receivers is not likely before the mid-eighties. Yet both will come, technically, with extraordinary effects on all existing national and local systems, subject always to political decisions. A very likely development is the linking of satellite television via ground stations to cable systems. These may well be the first 'multinational' – more strictly para-national – television corporations.

(*v*) Video-cassette production and distribution is already well under way. In its first stages it will bear the relation to television broadcasting that records have borne to concerts and radio. But as the market is expanded it seems certain that there will be, in addition to the cheaper forms of video-recording of already transmitted television programmes, some production of special-ised video-cassettes. There will be an alternative, here, between cassette production and demand-cable library-catalogue services. Meanwhile, movie cartridge projectors are being intensively developed.

(*vi*) Comparatively low-cost videotape recording equipment has already arrived, and is beginning to be quite extensively used for a different kind of television production, in community experiments and radical cultural enterprises. This could be rapidly extended, technically, but in general it serves a set of radically different interests from large-screen, satellite and cassette production. However, it has interesting practicable links with certain uses of cable television, especially in independent community stations.

(*vii*) Perhaps the most revolutionary technical developments are in the area of interactive television. It is already possible in some cable systems to respond to programmes in certain pre-determined ways: choosing an item from a shop display or from an advertisement, for example. There are already plans in the United States for instantaneous audience reaction to pro-grammes being transmitted; it has even been suggested that at a certain point in a play viewers could choose, by majority vote, whether it should have a 'sad' or a 'happy' ending. Audience measurement will in any case become a more accurate and virtually instantaneous procedure, by use of the reactive tech-nology now available. It is clear that the use of button-pressing reactive equipment would enable many kinds of choice to be made quickly and accurately; it is for example a perfectly possible voting procedure, given certain technically available safeguards.

But we have to distinguish between reactive and interactive technology. Nearly all the equipment that is being currently developed is reactive; the range of choices, both in detail and in scope, is pre-set. This will, undoubtedly, be very widely used.

More genuinely interactive television would depend on cable systems with associated special equipment. But there is an area of developing technology which allows for something between pre-set reaction and full interaction. This is a development from a technical possibility which is already being used to increase channel capacity. Between normal television signals there is a normally unseen and inaudible gap. An adapter fitted to an ordinary set can receive information or another programme transmitted during these signal gaps in an ordinary programme; the subliminal programme can then be played back on its own. Work is now going on in the United States to develop equipment for using the signal-gap for reaction-interaction, especially in educational programmes (there will of course be many normal educational programmes of a pre-set reaction, teaching-machine type).

B. INSTITUTIONS OF THE NEW TECHNOLOGY

It is clear that some of these technical developments taken singly, and certainly all of them taken together, will have a radical effect on all the institutions of television. We can first look at the effects of each kind of development taken separately.

(*i*) *New types of receiver:* these will mainly strengthen the existing large-network television institutions which, as in the case of colour, will undoubtedly develop programmes to promote and exploit them. But their cost, especially in the case of large-screen receivers, may open the way to other kinds of institution which are now pressing hard to get in. They might be associated, for example, with pay-television systems; there is already an American company offering first-run feature films by direct on-the-spot subscription, and the large screen would be especially useful for this. Monopoly transmission, by subscription, of many national and international sporting events is another probability.

(*ii*) *Cable systems:* these, undoubtedly, form the first major area of controversy, for a number of organisations, of different kinds, are ready to use cable technology to weaken or even to break the relative monopoly of the large-network broadcasting authorities. The irony is that the best-financed cable companies are offering what is, essentially, a version of the very worst kind of broadcasting service. It is not uncommon for a 12-channel cable system to be planned to carry nothing but old movies or old television entertainment series. The choice which is offered as a fruit of the new technology is a choice only within this repetitive dimension. The real motive, of course, is profit through advertising, but if this kind of cable television captured a significant share of advertising money, the funds available for production within the existing system would be considerably reduced. It is improbable, given the costs of cable-laying, that there would be much competition between cable systems, even in large cities. Moreover, commercial cable systems would concentrate on the cities and on areas of dense population. The reduction of available funds for ordinary broadcasting could thus lead to a reversal of some of the real social benefits of a broadcasting service. Moreover, even within cities, cable service would be selective by income. A Mitre Corporation analysis (*Urban Cable Systems*; William F. Mason, 1971) showed that maximum profit would be obtained at about 50 per cent coverage, while a Rand Corporation study (*Cable Communications in the Dayton Miami Valley*; L. L. Johnson, 1972) showed high profit on 40 per cent coverage, at a relatively high subscription fee, and predicted that lowering the subscription, while increasing coverage, would reduce the profit rate. Given the bias of such systems to advertising, itself seeking relatively affluent viewers, a commercial cable system would not really provide a community service, though there would usually be some time set aside for local information and services as a way of gaining prestige or consent. It might, rather, take over a significant part of general television entertainment service, with radical effects on general broadcasting. In the British system, where public service television is financed by licence fees, it is easy to imagine the campaign against licences which could be mounted when many viewers could get much of their television from a service financed by advertising or a service to which they were already subscribing at about the rate of a licence.

For all these reasons the existing broadcasting establishment is hostile to cable television, and the real social situation is then profoundly contradictory and paradoxical. For cable systems of a different kind, genuinely run by and serving local communities, with access to a full range of public programmes for which the necessary resources had been specifically provided, could indeed democratise broadcasting. This argument for democracy, for local needs, for freedom of reception and access, supports cable television as a technology. It would be a way of diminishing the power of remote and centralised broadcasting corporations, with their typical dependence on large capital or on state control or appointment. Similar arguments will indeed be used by the existing cable companies and their friends, but hypocritically, for locally controlled systems are the last thing they want, and community service, in their mouths, means consumer penetration. Yet the necessary opposition to that kind of cable system development could very easily turn into an uncritical defence of the existing large broadcasting corporations.

This problem can be resolved only if we realise that the cable system is indeed no more than a technology, and that every argument about it depends on its highly variable institutions and on the consequently variable links between cable distribution and other forms of service and production. All that needs to be re-emphasised now is that in its most common forms, in the companies which have the finance and the technology available, cable television is an extreme form of the earliest definition of broadcasting as simple *transmission*. Its extensive development, by the criteria of these companies, would gravely damage television *production*. Yet we are already able to see, from some publicly financed local experiments, that cable technology could alter the whole social and cultural process of televised communications.

(iii) *Visual information systems:* these are certain to be developed, though of course unevenly, as utilities. But if their profits are to go to private companies or to state agencies, there will again be some effect on the resources available for any planned public television and visual-information service of a co-ordinated kind.

(iv) *Satellite communications:* these systems, potentially, could have the greatest impact on existing institutions, for in one very probable kind of development they will be used to penetrate or circumvent existing national broadcasting systems, in the name of 'internationalism' but in reality in the service of one or two dominant cultures. Complicated and inconclusive international negotiations on the use of satellite television have already taken place. The two nations which could now mount a global satellite service, the United States and the Soviet Union, would have much to lose (though, temptingly, also much to gain) by a system of beaming television into each other's territories. The signs are that they will reach a stand-off agreement to leave each other's territories alone, but there is then still the problem of the rest of the world. It is probable that agreement will be reached that in international law the concept of national sovereignty will include the right to refuse beamed satellite signals. There are, after all, simple practical means of control, for a decade or so ahead, when reception could mainly depend on ground-stations, which can exercise selection or censorship. Alternatively, as in the European Broadcasting Union project, the satellite would have 12-channel narrow-beam transmission which, in favourable geographical circumstances, would transmit only to the areas of particular nation states.

When cheaper domestic satellite receivers become available, the conflict will become more open. Greater sensitivity in the receivers or, as probably, greater power in the satellite trans-mitters (though by a factor of ten, which is still some way to go) could enable people to get reception well beyond their frontiers. Smaller nations would have either to ban such receivers or accept what will be called the open sky. But even before that, in many poor countries, and in many medium-sized nations, where in varying degrees the costs of an independent national television service already present serious problems, there will be strong pressure to accept what will look like manna. In capitalist countries, especially, and in the third world, apparently national or local services, often funded by para-national corporations, could be set up, using their own ground-stations and cable systems, or their own satellite receivers, to offer comparatively cheap television which would have almost wholly originated outside the country. This would have important political and cultural effects, as already in the dumping of old series, or the penetrative promotion of current series, by the American corporations. Already many smaller societies, especially those on the borders of larger societies, are powerless to resist technical broadcast penetration. The primary motive of the operation, then as now, would be the penetration by para-national corporation advertising. The profits from this would be the factor making the service locally cheap, and in the course of time it could be very favourably competitive with all independent national systems.

Here again there is a paradox. A world-wide television service, with genuinely open skies, would be an enormous gain to the peoples of the world, as short-wave radio, bypassing national controls, has already clearly been. Against the rhetoric of open skies, which in fact, given the expense and sophistication of satellite technology, would be monopolised by a few large corporations and authoritarian governments, it will sound strange and reactionary to defend national autonomy. But the probable users of the technology are not internationalists, in the sense of any significant mutuality. The national or local components in their services would be matters merely of consent and publicity: tokenism. In most countries, if these systems gained control, independent production would become very difficult or impossible. Most of the inhabitants of the 'global village' would be saying nothing, in these new terms, while a few powerful corporations and governments, and the people they could hire, would speak in ways never before known to most of the peoples of the world.

There is still some time before this situation becomes critical. The major problems will arise in the 1980s. But the international negotiations so far conducted have been unimpressive. An international supervisory body, which could not only protect all nations' interests but also actively promote genuine international interchange, has so far been blocked by the relative monopoly of satellite technology and the consequent demands for weighted voting. Yet it remains an urgent need.

(v) *Cassettes:* in the early seventies video-cassettes have been mainly selling to institutions; a new general market drive is now about to open. In its early stages it will not greatly affect existing institutions; it will serve as a domestic ancillary, which many people will find useful. Behind this innocent front, more significant developments are already occurring. Links are being made between television production companies, publishers and cassette manufacturers. A situation could arise where with access to backlog material and with technical monopoly for educational contracts a new centre of production and distribution would acquire international significance. Some of these financial moves have as their objective the circumvention of existing national television systems and regulations, and the creation, within these monopoly terms, of an international video-consumer market. The irony is again that the cassette, as a technology, offers opportunities of a quite different kind: not only for individual use – seeing a programme when you want it, having a private cassette library – but for new 'publishing' institutions: small independent production companies, offering cassette programmes in ways similar to book-publishing before the monopoly tendencies of the sixties; larger public and semi-public production companies, offering a 'public library' cassette service. But as in every other phase of current development of the new technology, the interests (often protected by patents) which are now in charge have quite different ends in view.

(vi) *Videotape equipment:* this will be marketed as a domestic sideline (though for very well-off people), but it offers extraordinary opportunities for the development of independent community and educational television. Most of the centralisation of broadcasting arose from high capital costs. There are already enough examples of successful local experiments in video-making to encourage us to believe that the availability of this equipment may make a significant contribution to genuinely popular television. However, this will have to exist and survive in a world in which all the other technical tendencies are in an opposite direction, and it is then not so much a matter of costs alone, but of the effect of available models and expectations in what people produce for themselves.

(vii) *Reactive and interactive devices:* here, clearly, there are sharply alternative possible effects on the institutions. The technology has clear possibilities in community information and politics, and outstandingly in certain kinds of education. The main use that will be funded, however, unless some political change very quickly occurs, will be commercial. Advertising agencies are already deep in its techniques and possibilities. What matters, here, is how the necessary consoles are designed and how the computers will be controlled and programmed. Most signs now are that the effective definition will be of people as reactive consumers.

Any of the developments noted would, in itself, have some measurable effect on existing television institutions and policies. Cable, satellites and cassettes will have major effects. But it is only when we consider them in combination that we get some notion of the true scale of the problem. Consider, for example, the combination of a satellite, cable and cassette service, or of a broad-beam satellite service with augmented receivers. It would be para-national, financed by para-national corporation advertising, with cable distribution systems or manufacturing subsidiaries in many countries. It would command funds which would drive out of competition, from other kinds of service, most general entertainment, including backlog, many international news services, and almost all international sport, which would be tied in by sponsorship and monopoly contracts. There might well be two or three competing monopolies on this giant scale, though there are strong reasons against this, in satellite costs, and in the relative monopoly of ground-station and cable-distribution systems. There would be choice *within* such a system, but choice on its terms. It is of course perfectly possible – indeed there are already signs of this in the United States – that with majority television taken care of in this way, marginal systems would grow up: a limited educational service, limited national 'cultural' services, a cultural underground using its own video equipment. The major system would be so dominant that governments might be forced to 'rescue' a few things from it: education or minority programmes – a service at the level of a few publicly-financed universities, galleries or museums. Despising the system, the cultural and political radicals would develop their own local community and cultural alternatives. These exceptions would be very much better than nothing. But the social and cultural definitions of the best of broadcasting would have been decisively left behind.

C. ALTERNATIVE USES

We have always to remember that full development of the new video technology will take some twenty years: say between now and 1990. For this reason, some people, especially in the established authorities, manage to feel fairly relaxed about it: the problems will be sorted out as we go; it is no use trying to cross bridges before we come to them. But this is wrong on two main counts. First, some of the most serious problems will arise within the next few years: notably in relation to policies for cable television. Secondly, the history of broadcasting institutions shows very clearly that the institutions and social policies which get established in a formative, innovative stage – often *ad hoc* and piecemeal in a confused and seemingly marginal area – have extraordinary persistence into later periods, if only because they accumulate techniques, experience, capital or what come to seem prescriptive rights. The period of social decision has then to begin now.

In Britain this is especially the case, since the existing charters of mainstream broadcasting have to be renewed or revised within the next two or three years. In the United States the crisis of public television similarly requires immediate campaigns and decisions. And since within this exact period some of the key decisions about cable and satellites will have to be made – in the United States by the Federal Communications Commission, in Britain by the Minister and the Post Office – there has never been, and is unlikely to be in the future, a more suitable time for a general reconstruction of communications policies.

The politics of these decisions will be exceptionally complicated. It will be widely argued that the old choice between 'public service' and 'commercial' broadcasting is now outdated by the new technology, and that we can move beyond both to community services. This is to some extent true, but 'community service', in this confused argument, will turn out on examination to mean radically different things, and the choice between them can still best be expressed as a choice between public service and commercial development. However, if, in the course of the argument, we can make a further distinction between 'public service' of a traditional kind, controlled by appointed central authorities, and 'public service' of a new kind, controlled democratically by local communities and by those who work in the institutions, a new range of social possibility will have been opened. It may even turn out that the public-service institutions can only be saved from their probable defeat or absorption by the new international commercial institutions if they can themselves be reformed into fully democratic and experimental enterprises.

For many years yet, central programming and networking authorities are going to continue. They must become or continue as public authorities, expressing the concept of the airwaves as public property. But it would be wise to look again at the question which is still unresolved from the earliest days of broadcasting: the relation between transmission and production. In all current systems too few people are making the primary decisions about production. The real need is for more independent production companies, which would be given publicly protected contracts with the programming and networking authorities. It would not be an easy system to devise and administer, but it is the only creative social course to take between the existing monopolies and their new challengers. Moreover it offers a model for the solution of the problem of cable-television institutions. At a national level cable facilities, like the airwaves, must be conceived as public property, and the operation of these facilities, by any group to which licence has been given, must be part of the system of publicly protected contracts between the cable operators and production companies. In many cases there could be permanent links, in particular communities, between local public-owned cable companies and production companies: real local bases from which some material would pass into one or other of the networks. At the same time it would be necessary to have some specialised national production companies: alternative providers of national and international news and public affairs programmes; educational and arts companies; a central library and information video-service. These would be necessary to accompany the main emphasis, in cable policy, on community stations. The community emphasis is so right, in its own terms, and could so notably contribute to solving the problems of urban information flow, democratic discussion and decision-making and community identity, that it is easy to overlook the dimension that is inevitably there, beyond the community – the nation and the world with which it is inevitably involved. The back-up national and international services would protect community television from its greatest danger: that its legitimate sense of locality will leave a gap which will be exploited by wholly irresponsible institutions beyond it.

The political problems must then again be stressed. First, community is a word that will be exploited by commercial operators and by the political enemies of the now partly independent programming and networking authorities. But a community is also a real social fact: not an idealised notion but a social system containing radical inequalities and conflicts of interest. Judging from all previous experience, nothing will be easier, for the national and international commercial operators, than to sign up local community representatives. I say 'sign up';

the real terms are buy or hire. It will be treated as a 'dealership', 'outlet' or 'appointed agency' problem, as now with Toyota or Esso. Again and again, unless it is specifically prevented, 'community' stations will be mere fronts for irresponsible networks which have their real centres elsewhere. There is no solution to this problem but to make local communications ownership and control subject to open and democratic local process, with specific provisions against financing, salary payments and consultancies from outside commercial bodies. The political fight to achieve that will be long and bitter, but it is better to face it than to be deluded by the public-relations version of 'local community' which major capitalist interests are already circulating.

The same point applies when the 'local community' is what is still thought of as the independent national state. In the third world, but also very clearly even in Western Europe, for all its residual national prides, the real political situation already is that many so-called national agencies are in fact or in effect branch offices of international capitalist corporations. American corporations, especially, have been skilful and persistent in these kinds of penetration and hiring, and there is never any shortage of local people, local nationals, willing to be penetrated or hired. Since this process further extends, in whole or in part, to governments and political parties, it can be seen that it is not enough to make simple appeals to national authorities to act in the public interest. On the contrary, only independent democratic organisations – themselves engaged in just this kind of struggle over a very wide field – can honestly engage with the problems. But for this they need information, publicity, sustained campaigning: much of it necessarily in the areas and in the channels which are in dispute, and where, in too many cases, their hired enemies are already firmly established. The battle for free communications is then necessarily part of a much wider social struggle, but that is no reason for abstaining from struggle, from proposal and counter-proposal, on each and every issue as it arises.

Legislation on foreign agencies, in the whole field of communications, is then a necessary and urgent objective. What is already a serious situation will have become virtually irretrievable by the 1980s, unless very strong action is taken. In another dimension, there must be continual pressure for proper international agreements on satellite television, in particular refusing all control bodies with weighted voting, since these in practice would mean control by the superpowers. Smaller nations may seem to have little to bargain with, but while they retain control over ground-stations and over foreign or foreign-hired broadcasting or cable distribution systems, they are in fact in a strong position. The positive position in these negotiations can then be the institution of international and transnational television systems under democratic international agencies.

All this will take time and prolonged effort. The struggle will reach into every corner of society. But that is precisely what is at stake: a new universal accessibility. Over a wide range from general television through commercial advertising to centralised information and data-processing systems, the technology that is now or is becoming available can be used to affect, to alter, and in some cases to control our whole social process. And it is ironic that the uses offer such extreme social choices. We could have inexpensive, locally based yet internationally extended television systems, making possible communication and information-sharing on a scale that not long ago would have seemed utopian. These are the contemporary tools of the long revolution towards an educated and participatory democracy, and of the recovery of effective communication in complex urban and industrial societies. But they are also the tools of what would be, in context, a short and successful counter-revolution, in which, under the cover of talk about choice and competition, a few para-national corporations, with their attendant states and agencies, could reach farther into our lives, at every level from news to psycho-drama, until individual and collective response to many different kinds of experience and problem became almost limited to choice between their programmed possibilities.

There is good reason to believe that many people will resist this worst of developments, but as the size of effective decision-taking communities gets so much larger, and as the scale and complexity of interlocking agencies makes identification let alone struggle more difficult, it is not enough to rely on unaided virtues. Within the next few years, decisions will be taken or will fail to be taken which will to a large extent determine which of these possible roads we are likely to take, for the remainder of this century. But if action is necessary now, its first conditions are information, analysis, education, discussion, to which this book is offered as a small contribution and, it is hoped, an incentive.

Major idea of f conspiracy theory Sees institutions as faceless quantities, with a life of their own rather than ~~operated~~ people working en masse

Selected Bibliography

ACTT. *Fortyeight times the usual junk*. London, 1973
Arons, L. *Television and Human Behaviour*. New York, 1963
Bakewell, J. and Garnham, N. *The New Priesthood: British Television Today*. London, 1970
Barnouw, E. *A History of Broadcasting in the United States*.
             Vol. 1: A Tower in Babel
             Vol. 2: The Golden Web
             Vol. 3: The Image Empire
                                 Oxford, 1966–70
Belsen, W. A. *The Impact of Television*. Hamden, Conn., 1967
Black, P. *The Mirror in the Corner*. London, 1972
Blumler, J. and McQuail, D. *Television in Politics*. London, 1968
Bogart, L. *The Age of Television: a study of viewing habits*. New York, 1972
Briggs, A. *The Birth of Broadcasting*. London, 1961
Brown, L. *Television: the business behind the box*. New York, 1971
Center for Policy Research. *Minerva: a study in Participatory Technology*. Working Paper, 1972
Council, C. *From Circuits to Circus: daily TV*. New York, 1970
De Forest, L. *Television now and onwards*. London, 1946
Dubin, R. *The medium may be related to the message*. Univ. Oregon, 1965
Dunlap, O. E. *Understanding Television*. New York, 1948
Dyer, R. *Light Entertainment* (BFI). London, 1973
Efron, E. *The News Twisters*. Los Angeles, 1971
Eguchi, H. *International Studies in Broadcasting*. NHK, 1971

Emery, W. B. *National and International Systems of Broadcasting*. Michigan, 1969

Everson, G. *The Story of Television*. New York, 1949

Fekete, J. *A Theoretical Critique of some aspects of North American critical theory*. (Ph.D. thesis, Cambridge, 1972)

Feldman, N. E. *Cable television: opportunities and problems*. Santa Monica, 1970

Feshbach, S. *Television and Aggression*. San Francisco, 1971

Fielding, R. *A technological history of motion pictures and television*. Berkeley, 1967

Garnham, N. *Structures of Television* (BFI). London, 1973

Garvey, D. E. *Social Control in the television newsroom*. (Thesis, Stanford)

Green, T. *The Universal Eye*. New York, 1972

Greenberg, B. S. *Use of the mass media by the urban poor*. New York, 1970

Groombridge, B. *Television and the People*. London, 1972

Halloran, J. *Effects of Mass Communication*. Leicester, 1964

Halloran, J. (ed.) *Effects of Television*. London, 1970

Halloran, J. D., Brown, R. L., and Chaney, D. *Television and Delinquency*. Leicester, 1970

Hazard, P. D. (ed.) *Television as Art*. National Council of Teachers of English, USA, 1966

Heath, R. *Radio and Television*. London, 1969

Himmelweit, H. T., Oppenheim, A. N., and Vince, P. *Television and the Child*. London, 1958

Hubbell, R. W. *4000 years of television*. New York, 1942

Innis, H. *Empire and Communications*. Oxford, 1950

International Broadcasting Convention. *Report*. London, 1970

Janky, J. M. *Optimisation in design of mass-production microwave receiver suitable for direct reception from satellites*. (Thesis, Stanford, 1971)

Johnson, L. L. *Cable television and question of protecting local broadcasting*. Santa Monica, 1970

Johnson, L. L. *The future of cable television; some problems of federal regulation*. Santa Monica, 1970

Johnson, L. L. *Cable TV and higher education.* Santa Monica, 1971

Johnson, N. *How to talk back to your TV set.* Boston, 1970

Kirschner, A. and L. *Radio and Television.* New York, 1971

Klavan, G. *Turn that damned thing off.* Indianapolis, 1972

Kuroki, S. *An analysis of modulation techniques for wideband FM television system.* (Stanford, 1972)

Lackman, R. *Remember TV?* New York, 1971

Lichty, L. *World and International Broadcasting: a bibliography.* New York, 1971

Maddox, B. *Beyond Babel.* London, 1972

Mayer, M. *About television.* New York, 1972

McLuhan, M. *Understanding Media.* New York, 1964

Mickleson, S. *The electric mirror: politics in the age of television.* New York, 1972

Mitre Corporation. *Cable Television: Report.* 1972

Morris, N. S. *Television's child.* Boston, 1971

National Citizens' Committee. *The State of Public Broadcasting.* New York, 1968

Park, R. E. *Potential Impact of Cable growth on television broadcasting.* Santa Monica, 1970

Park R. E. *Cable television and UHF broadcasting.* Santa Monica, 1971

Parker, E. B. *Assessment and Control of Communication Technology.* (Stanford, 1972)

Pilkington Report. London, 1962

Postmaster-General. *Report of Television Committee.* London, 1935

Radical Software, 1970–71. (New York)

Ross, G. *TV Jubilee.* London, 1961

Rotha, P. *Television in the making.* London, 1956

Schiller, H. I. *Mass Communications & American Empire.* New York, 1970

Shapiro, P. D. *Networking in Cable Television.* (Stanford, 1972)

Shayon, R. L. *Open to Criticism.* Boston, 1971

Skolnik, R. *A bibliography of selected publications in foreign and international broadcasting.* Michigan, 1966

Skornia, H. J. *Television and Society*. New York, 1965

Skornia, H. J. and Kitson, J. W. *Problems and Controversies in television and radio* (basic readings). Palo Alto, 1968

Small, W. J. *To kill a messenger: TV news and the real world*. New York, 1970

Stanford Institute for Communication Research. *Educational television: the next ten years*. Stanford, 1962

Stavens, R. L. (ed.) *Television today: the end of communication and death of community*. Washington, 1969, 1971

Steiner, G. A. *The people look at television: a study of audience attitudes*. New York, 1963

Summers, R. E. *Broadcasting and the Public*. Belmont, 1966

Surgeon-General's Scientific Advisory Committee. *Television and Growing Up*. Washington, 1972

Taggart, R. B. *Instructional TV via satellite*. (Thesis, Stanford, 1970)

Tate, C. (ed.) *Cable TV in the Cities*. New York, 1972

Thomson, R. *TV crime drama: its impact on children and adolescents*. Melbourne, 1959

UNESCO. *World Radio and Television*. New York, 1965

UNESCO. *Communications in the Space Age: the use of satellites by the mass media*. Paris, 1968

Wedell, E. G. *Broadcasting and Public Policy*. London, 1968

Wedell, E. G. (ed.) *Structures of Broadcasting*. Manchester, 1970

Weil, G. L. (ed.) *Communicating by Satellite: an international discussion*. New York, 1969

Wells, A. F. *Picture-tube Imperialism*. New York, 1972

Williams, R. *Communications*. London, 1966

Wolf, F. *Television programming for news and public affairs*. New York, 1972

Worsley, T. C. *Television the ephemeral art*. London, 1970

Index